THE
STUDENT SOLDIERS

by

JOHN McCONACHIE

Printed and Published by
MORAVIAN PRESS LTD.
31 SOUTH STREET ELGIN MORAY IV30 ILA
1995

For my grandchildren
IAIN and CATRIONA McCONACHIE
whose great grandfather
fought in the Great War

FOREWORD

In the archives of the University of Aberdeen, covering the period from the turn of the century up to the outbreak of the Great War in 1914, there are frequent references to 'U' Company. To the graduate and undergraduate of those long-forgotten days, 'U' Company was something intimately bound up with the social and corporate life of their Alma Mater. For the graduate and undergraduate of today, the story of this heroic Company is largely unknown.

The soldier-diarists of the Great War are well-documented, and many personal diaries have found their way into print. This Aberdeen unit – 'U' Company, or more properly, the University of Aberdeen Company of the 4th Battalion of the Gordon Highlanders – had at least seven diarists in the ranks of the students and graduates of the University who made up that Company and whose efforts have survived the passage of the years. Although this book is written principally around the diary of John Knowles MA, the author has also had access to the diaries, letters and writings of James Anderson, Robert Donald MA, James Fraser MA, MB ChB, and Alexander Rule MA, BSc, who were all members of the Company. Their diaries and letters are significant historical documents in which the writers record their thoughts and feelings and experiences on a day to day basis, and they paint a vivid picture of the life of an infantryman in the early days of the Great War.

The published and unpublished letters, diaries and books of the Great War range from the light-hearted to serious – and often depressing – accounts of life in and out of the trenches. A small number may have been meant for publication but the great majority of diaries were a simple record of their owner's reactions to a new and, at intervals, quite terrifying experience. These diaries provide an intimate picture of intelligent young men, like the rest of their companions in U Company, thrown into a situation for which nothing had prepared them. This could only be made tolerable to a degree by the comradeship of their friends and the shared knowledge of the life they had left and to which they hoped shortly to return. They patently did not relish what they were about to endure, but like so many young men at the time they saw it as an obligation and a patriotic duty which had to be undertaken, even at the cost of their young lives. It is fitting that these accounts should appear soon after the 200th anniversary of the founding of the Gordon Highlanders, and on the Quincentenary of the University at which they had been students.

First published 1995
© John McConachie 1995
ISBN 1 870151 05 4

Reproduction of the photographic prints on pages 7, 9, 20, 34 and 67 by permission
of the George Washington Wilson Collection, Aberdeen University Library.
Photographic print on page 43 by courtesy of the Imperial War Museum.

CONTENTS

INTRODUCTION

by

Lieutenant General Sir Peter Graham KCB CBE

This is a book written with great skill and feeling about a very special, unique group of Gordon Highlanders - U Company, 4th Gordons. Rarely if ever has such a talented group of men served together at sub-unit level. Rarely can there have been such a loss of intelligent, humane, men of character in a small unit, and of course the effect of that loss has been felt greatly in succeeding generations in the North East of Scotland. But what a moving story is contained in this book. It is made all the more poignant through the diaries and letters of the officers and men who served in the Company and in the 4th Battalion of the Regiment; men like Private John Knowles MA, Private Alexander Rule MA, BSc, Private James Anderson, Corporal James Fraser MA, MB ChB, Captain Norman Down and others. It seems very fitting that their voices should be heard again in 1995, the year after their proud Regiment was amalgamated on completing 200 years of service, the year of the Quincentenary of their beloved University and the eightieth year after the battle which destroyed so many of them.

Unfortunately I am not a graduate. Had I gone to University it would have been to Aberdeen for my education began at Fyvie Village School in Aberdeenshire. However, my father, a doctor from Aberdeen whom I admired greatly and who is mentioned in this book, and my beloved wife Alison were both medical graduates of the University. So it is a particular pleasure and a great honour for me to be asked by Dr John McConachie to write the Introduction, both from a family and Regimental point of view. Sadly I am the last Colonel, The Gordon Highlanders: 'last' because of the amalgamation that took place in September 1994.

All Gordon Highlanders and all those connected with the University of Aberdeen owe a debt of gratitude to John McConachie for the research, scholarship and sheer hard work he has put into producing this book. He has uncovered the history of this legendary band of Gordon Highlanders. They were clever, talented men, many from humble backgrounds, who believed that their duty to their King, Country and Regiment came before self. Indeed they wanted to serve as Private Soldiers rather than in any other capacity because the comradeship was strong, close knit and mattered. They showed extraordinary courage, true service, sacrifice, teamwork, steadfastness and humour, often making light of the difficulties they faced while getting on steadily with the job in hand. These attitudes, brought out so clearly in this book, are among the attributes that made The Gordon Highlanders world famous.

The book also gives a wonderful insight into the life led by the junior ranks in the early days of the First World War. The unimaginative training and lack of proper tactical exercises, the extraordinary emphasis on interior economy, the paucity of time spent on developing shooting skills or musketry as it was called, the poor administration, the lack of communication, the horror of the trenches, are all made clear. While, on the other side of the coin, one cannot help but be moved by the commitment, comradeship, enthusiasm, patriotism and courage of the members of U Company, 4th Gordons. Indeed one is also struck by their obvious love of their own families, friends and their native airt.

As I have said already there is a great deal to be learned from this excellent book by John McConachie. Above all it is the understanding of the characteristics and attitudes of a body of men, from a wonderful part of the world, whose Regiment was described by Winston Churchill, once Rector of the University of Aberdeen, as ' the finest Regiment in the World'.

ACKNOWLEDGEMENTS

This book would not have been published without the financial assistance of the Aberdeen Medico-Chirurgical Society and I am indebted to the members of the Society, and their President Dr Alan Milne, for promoting this work. The help and encouragement of Past-Presidents Dr William R Gauld and Dr Alfred W Raffan, and the present librarian Mr Alexander Adam FRCS, is gratefully acknowledged and their enthusiastic support has made this publication possible.

The research for this monograph encompassed visits to the Imperial War Museum, the British Library Newspaper Library at Colindale, the Public Record Office at Kew, the Public Libraries at Bedford, Aberdeen and Elgin, the headquarters of the University of Aberdeen Officers Training Corps and the Archives at King's College in Aberdeen. The staffs of these institutions were invariably pleasant and helpful but I would like to mention Graeme Wilson of the Elgin Library for his unfailing courtesy and co-operation. I have to thank Captain Jim Easson of the University OTC and Captain Colin Harrison of the Regimental Headquarters of the Gordon Highlanders at Aberdeen for their generous assistance. My Morayshire friends Douglas Craib, Lt-Colonel Grenville Johnston, Ian Keillar, David Mackessack-Leitch, Dr Gordon Milne, Lt-Colonel Neil Simpson, Charles Wilken, and that redoubtable Seaforth Lachlan McIntosh, all assisted me in various ways, as did Ian Edward, the Reverend George Skakle, Alan Pattillo and W D Campbell of Toronto.

Many relatives of the members of U Company provided original material and photographs and were generous in their assistance. I am indebted to Mrs Margaret Bruce of Aberdeen for access to the letters of James Anderson, and for making available to me the fruits of her own research into U Company. John G N Fraser of Aberdeen and Edward Fraser of Edinburgh, the sons of Dr James Fraser, not only allowed me to make use of their father's writings but also provided photographs and commented on the text. Dr Robin Donald of Aberdeen sent me his father's diary and photographs of the Company at Tain and Mrs Margaret Allan of Edinburgh confirmed the story of her father at Zillebeke and allowed me to use his photograph. Arthur Crichton's son Bill produced many photographs and Sandy Gibb of Elgin proved a willing and reliable courier. Mr John Rule Philip of Aberchirder very generously gave me his uncle's papers and diaries and his copy of *Students Under Arms* with the original dust cover which is reproduced in the text. My debt to Sandy Rule's writings is obvious.

David Hamilton FRCS, of Kilmacolm, the distinguished golf historian, read the manuscript at every stage and offered much invaluable advice. My brother, Dr Allan McConachie, took many photographs and applied his computer skills to the construction of the index, while James Wilson of Lossiemouth helped me to overcome my difficulties with a computer. I am especially grateful to the historian Dr A J Peacock of York, the editor of *Gunfire, A Journal of First World War History*, for his comments on a late draft of this book. My wife, Dr Margaret McConachie, read the manuscript repeatedly and made many helpful suggestions.

My thanks are due to the University of Aberdeen for reducing their photographic reproduction fees, to the Imperial War Museum for waiving their fee, and to the family of the late Eric Linklater for kindly allowing me to use excerpts and illustrations from *Fanfare For a Tin Hat*.

PREFACE

The first official reference to the formation of U Company of the Gordon Highlanders is in the University of Aberdeen students' magazine *Alma Mater* account of a general meeting of the Company held in Marischal College on Thursday 27 October 1898. Captain W O Duncan, the students' Company Commander, presided and reviewed the previous year's training. In his remarks he stated that the attendances at the ordinary Battalion training, at shooting practice and at the annual camp had all been unsatisfactory and he attributed the poor turnout to the fact that students were not enrolled as a separate Company in the Battalion. The following motions were then submitted to the meeting.

1 The meeting resolved to ask the Officer Commanding the 1st Volunteer Battalion of the Gordon Highlanders to enrol University Students in a separate Company; and to order that students matriculated in any one year be alone eligible to join, or serve as NCOs of that Company. After discussion, this was passed unanimously.

2 The matriculated students, enrolled members of the 1st VBGH, resolved to form themselves into a Club, and passed these Rules:-

    1 Name - Aberdeen University Gordon Highlanders Club.

    2 Membership - Confined to matriculated students, past or present, serving as Volunteers.

    3 Office-Bearers and Committee - Five elected NCOs, 1st VBGH, and four privates, one elected from each year, along with the Officers of the Company.

    4 Objects - Athletics and Shooting.

A Committee was then appointed, and five secretaries were appointed to each of the sub-committees – General, Shooting, Amusements, Gymnastics and Ambulance.

Following this meeting, the newly formed Gordon Highlanders Club applied for and was admitted to membership of the University Athletic Association, enabling it to obtain grants for gymnastic classes.

On 10 November 1898, by Battalion Order of the 1st Volunteer Battalion of the Gordon Highlanders, a new Company, lettered 'U' Company, was formed for members of the Battalion who were students at the University. In this simple way a legend was born.

THE
STUDENT SOLDIERS

CHAPTER ONE

Prelude

THE obverse of one of the two medals (known as Mutt and Jeff) awarded to all those who served in the first Great War proclaimed it had been 'The Great War for Civilisation 1914-1919'. To those who took part in and survived that terrible struggle it did indeed seem that the fight was against the powers of darkness. Until late in the war, the principal cause of the incomprehensible disasters which happened to large groups of men and indeed whole armies seems to have been the lack of any rapidly effective means of communication between the soldiers on the battlefield and the generals commanding the operations.

This lack of communication can best be illustrated by the events on the first day of the Battle of the Somme on 1 July 1916. After many months of preparation and training, a huge continuous artillery barrage was launched about a week beforehand on the German troops in their forward trenches. At this stage in the fighting it was recognised that a prolonged artillery barrage was probably the most frightening and demoralising weapon of war – provided the enemy was not dug in far enough below ground to ensure his protection. This heavy and prolonged shell-fire had three purposes: to terrorise and to kill the defenders and to cut gaps in the barbed wire in front of the enemy trenches to allow the attacking troops through. There was a singular failure to achieve these objectives and the 13 divisions of British Tommies who advanced in close lines abreast at a walking pace were mown down in their thousands by concentrated machine-gun and rifle fire. On that first day of the battle alone the British losses were 19,000 dead and 38,000 wounded – this was to remain the greatest loss on one day by any side in the Great War. It is little wonder that for many years after the war the first of July was commemorated in households throughout the land by drawn curtains and the wearing of black armbands.

The late afternoon and evening London newspapers carried the first news of the British attack in the form of a message from the news agency Reuters.

British Headquarters in France, Saturday.

At about half-past seven this morning a vigorous
attack was launched by the British Army.
The front extends over about twenty miles north of the Somme.
The assault was preceded by a terrific bombardment
lasting about an hour and a half.
It is too early yet to give anything but the
barest particulars as the fighting is developing in
intensity, but the British troops have already
occupied the German front line.
Many prisoners have already fallen into our hands
and so far as can be ascertained our casualties have not been heavy.

1

This communiqué put out by General Headquarters in France showed that the General Staff and their Commander-in-Chief Field Marshal Haig had little or no knowledge of what was taking place on the battlefield, and this lack of communication in part explains many of the defeats and disasters which occurred during 1916 and 1917. This difference between the First World War and the Second World War is further illustrated by a report which was carried by *The Times* of 5 September 1916. This noted that some of the chief officials of the War Office had had a private viewing at the *Scala Theatre* [in London] of the official film *The Battle of the Somme* which was then on show to the public. The exhibition was given for the express purpose of showing the Chiefs of Staff the nature of the ground over which their soldiers had to fight, and the effect of different types of artillery upon trenches and dugouts.

At this stage of the war reconnaissance by air and aerial photography was in its infancy and this film of some of the Somme action, made from the trenches by Lieutenant Geoffrey Malins and J B McDowell, was at that time the sole available visual evidence of what happened, although the Staff could not have lacked first hand accounts from officers and NCOs who had taken part in the battle. The storm of criticism of staff officers who had never been near the front line culminated in the story which was said to concern General Sir Launcelot Kiggell – Haig's Chief of Staff until he had a nervous breakdown – being driven along the Menin Road to the muddy swamp of the battlefield of Passchendaele after the battle in 1917. 'My God', he is reputed to have said, 'did we really send men to fight in this'? 'It's much worse further up', replied the stony-faced battalion commander who was accompanying him.

One of the strange features of the Great War is that a huge civilian army was commanded entirely by senior officers who were all professional soldiers long before the war, many of whom had served in the Boer War at the turn of the century. Although many civilians of high intellectual ability found their way into the war-time army, few if any reached high command, and it is clear that their talents for war were never exploited because of the rigidities of the system. The same mistake was not to be made in the Second World War.

At another level this failure to use men of talent is illustrated by the story of a group of young men, the students and graduates of the University of Aberdeen who formed the University Company of the 4th Battalion of the Gordon Highlanders and who went to war as a unit in the year of 1914. They were the only university infantry company ever to do so. Three-quarters of U Company were arts students and the remainder were students from the faculties of law, science, medicine and agriculture. There were more than 50 graduates in the Company, 41 men in the ranks holding the degree of MA; 15 of them with honours degrees. This was without doubt the most highly educated infantry unit in the British Expeditionary Force and probably the most highly educated unit in the history of warfare.

The failure to recognise this combatant unit as an excellent source of potential officers is all the more remarkable since Haig himself, in November 1914, almost three months before U Company went to France, had suggested that the most fruitful source of officer material was the student bodies of the Universities of Oxford and Cambridge who would, as he put it, 'understand the crisis in which the British Empire is involved'. The necessity to find more officers in November of 1914, just four months after the start of the war, was due to the high number of casualties among the officers of the BEF which had gone to France to help the French against the German onslaught. The original British Expeditionary Force was a small professional army which lost a large number of its officers in the retreat of 1914, culminating in the battles in October and November commonly known as

First Ypres. Young men of intelligence with some military experience were required to replace these officers as a matter of urgency.

On 10 November 1913, one year before Haig's comments, Field Marshal Earl Roberts had written a letter to the students of the University of Aberdeen which was published prominently on the first page of *Alma Mater*. This edition devoted six full pages to military training at the University and contained a letter from the Principal, George Adam Smith, commending to students the various University Corps connected with the defence of the United Kingdom.

Message from Field Marshal Earl Roberts, VC

Englemere
Ascot, Berks.
10 November 1913

I am very glad that a special effort is being made at the University of Aberdeen to stimulate recruiting for the University Company of the Territorial Force and for the Officers' Training Corps.

The shortage of officers for our defensive forces is a most serious matter and one that must be faced and remedied.

I commend the movement to the students, and trust they will avail themselves of the opportunity afforded them to do a real service to their country by fitting themselves to fulfil the sacred duty of defending her in her hour of need.

Roberts F M

Origins of the University Company

The first military unit with which the University was associated was the Old Aberdeen Volunteers (1798-1802) which was commanded by the Rev Gilbert Gerard who was the Professor of Divinity at King's College, and whose father had been Professor of Theology. He had as his lieutenants the Rev William Jack, Vice-Principal and later Principal of King's College, and Professor Robert Scott who held the chair of Moral Philosophy. The Volunteers made their first public appearance in Aberdeen in October 1798 when they paraded in front of the Town House. There they fired three volleys, performed it was said with great exactness, to celebrate Admiral Nelson's victory over the French at the Battle of the Nile.

The Old Aberdeen Volunteers was one of the many units raised to meet the threat of a sea-borne invasion of the British Isles by the French. Britain headed a coalition of Prussia, Austria and other countries against France in the last phase of the long wars between Britain and France for colonial and maritime supremacy, which was in effect a conflict between two very different political systems. The great rallying cry of the French Revolution, *Liberty, Equality, Fraternity,* is today the motto of the French Republic. Of the three, equality was to the French man and woman of 1789 by far the most important. It meant the abolition of privileges enjoyed by aristocrats and the clergy who were exempt from taxation, the chief burden of taxation falling upon peasants, artisans, merchants and professional men.

The French revolution occurred when the funds in the national treasury had been exhausted by the ruinous wars and the extravagances of the weak and irresolute Louis XVI and his frivolous and spendthrift queen, Marie Antoinette. The storming of the Bastille on 14 July 1789 was the most symbolic event of the revolution and the King and his court were swept away and replaced by a republic. The French revolution was followed by a perceptible change in the British class system: an unease in the upper classes at the idea of equality, and a sharper insistence on distinction. This was most notable in the army and particularly so in the army in India, and by Rudyard Kipling's time in the late 19th century British officers and British other ranks had become so different that they were almost two races. The Indian empire was ruled by a specially trained class who even had their own public school – Haileybury College in Hertfordshire was created in 1805 by the directors of the East India Company to train future administrators for the Indian Civil Service. Boys were admitted to the school at the age of 15 and spent three years studying the classics, history, mathematics, natural philosophy, law and political economy. They also acquired some knowledge of oriental languages.

In March of 1802 the Old Aberdeen Volunteers presented their commandant Major Gerard with a very elegant piece of plate as a token of the esteem in which he was held, and in May the corps was 'disembodied' – in the military jargon of the day – and was never again re-embodied. Their colours were presented to the University of Aberdeen in 1884 and hung for many years in the chapel of King's College. In the early years of this century the drum of the same corps could be seen in the Town House in Aberdeen. It was a reminder of the days when public intimations of all kinds were made by the 'tuck' of the drum, the drummer being dressed in a uniform of red coat and tall hat.

The prospect of a French invasion again arose between 1803-08, when for a time 100,000 French soldiers were encamped at Boulogne, and French warships and transport boats were being built and readied. In Aberdeen the Finlason Fencibles, the Gilcomston Pikemen and the Aberdeen Pikemen were raised to combat the new threat, but the invasion did not materialise. Admiral Nelson again came to the rescue of Great Britain in 1805 by engaging and defeating both the French and Spanish fleets at Cape Trafalgar off the south-west coast of Spain. Nelson, on *HMS Victory*, was killed by a musket shot from the deck of the French ship *Redoubtable*, and his brother the Rev William Nelson was created a peer and given a pension of £5000 a year. This pension continued until 1946 when it was ended by the post-second war Labour government.

Long after the French had ceased to be a menace to Britain, voluntary service in the Army continued to have a strong attraction for young men, and the students of the University of Aberdeen resumed their part-time soldiering with the 1st Aberdeenshire Rifle Volunteers in 1860. In the same year Aberdeen ceased to have two independent Universities, and King's College and Marischal College, which had existed side by side for almost three centuries, became, by Act of Parliament, the University of Aberdeen. In 1883 the 1st Aberdeenshire Rifle Volunteers became the 1st Volunteer Battalion of the Gordon Highlanders.

The University Corps

The first military unit recruited solely from the University of Aberdeen was a company which was raised in 1885 attached to the Aberdeen Artillery Volunteers, and its commanding officer was Professor William Stirling who held the chair of Physiology from 1877-86. He was soon followed by Professor James W H Trail of the Botany Department who captained the unit for the next nine years until March of 1895 when the company was absorbed into the 1st Heavy Battery. The next commander was Herbert J C Grierson, Professor of English Literature from 1894-1915, and he was assisted by Professor J A MacWilliam of the chair of Physiology and Professor William M Ramsay who held the chair of Humanity.

The second Aberdeen University military unit was a Volunteer Medical Staff Corps which was formed as a direct result of Professor [Sir] Alexander Ogston's experiences as a military surgeon in the Egyptian campaign of 1884-85. Alexander Ogston held the chair of surgery in Aberdeen from 1882-1909 and had built himself a laboratory behind his house at 252, Union Street in Aberdeen where he carried out the research which was to make him famous. His name is hallowed – not only in Aberdeen but in medical circles throughout the world – as the man who discovered in 1880 that suppuration and the pus produced was due to a germ, the staphylococcus, so-called from the Greek for the bunch of grapes it resembled. This discovery had eluded both Koch and Lister and was derided by the editor of the *British Medical Journal* who asked scathingly, 'can any good thing come out of Aberdeen?' He did not get his answer until 100 years later in 1980 when an international conference on 'The Staphylococci' was held in Aberdeen, fittingly entitled 'The Alexander Ogston Centennial Conference'. Tetanus, gas-gangrene and wound infection with the staphylococcus were to lead to countless amputations and deaths among the wounded of the Great War for whom there were no antibiotics and very little blood transfusion.

Ogston had a great interest in military surgery and helped to found the Royal Army Medical Corps in 1898. His great predecessor Sir James McGrigor (1771-1858), another graduate of the University of Aberdeen, had spent his career in the Army working towards the same end. McGrigor was Director General of the Army Medical Department for 36 years from 1815-51 and the trusted adviser and confidant of the Duke of Wellington, but he did not live to see the formation of the RAMC. Professor Ogston was later involved in the Boer War and the Great War and from his diaries he wrote his book *Reminiscences of Three Campaigns* which was published in 1919. Until about 1887 doctors had been attached as medical officers to the various volunteer units, but the formation of an Ambulance Association Committee for Aberdeen in 1886 led to the creation of a Medical Staff Corps in 1889 which was composed entirely of medical students. This corps, commanded by Dr Alexander MacGregor, was over 100 strong and was included in Haldane's Territorial Force in 1908. Curiously enough the unit was inspected during three weeks training at Aldershot in 1889 by its future enemy Kaiser Wilhelm II, the grandson of Queen Victoria and the Emperor of Germany.

U Company

The Shooting Team - February 1899

5

The third Aberdeen University army unit was U Company, and membership was confined entirely to the students of the University of Aberdeen. In spite of this proviso, graduates of the university who had been members of U Company in their student days and had enjoyed the camaraderie and the annual camps continued to serve in the ranks – some of them long after they had started work in their chosen professions. This unit had its origins in the 1st Volunteer Battalion of the Gordon Highlanders. In 1897 a number of keen students joined the Woodside Company of that battalion and in a very short time student recruits began to enrol in considerable numbers. Woodside was at that time outwith the boundary of the city of Aberdeen and the Company was so-called because it recruited in that area. The students were fortunate to find themselves under the command of Captain W O Duncan, a graduate of the University of Cambridge and a noted oarsman. The keenness and enthusiasm of the students was not a sign of militarism on the model then prevalent in Germany; rather they were intent on defending their own country against attack.

In 1898 Colonel Douglass Duncan, an Aberdeen advocate, commanded the 1st Volunteer Battalion of the Gordons, and he was persuaded by the enthusiasm of the students to form a University Company from the student section of G (Woodside) Company. This new Company became an independent unit in the 1st Volunteer Battalion, and as such it soon became known as one of the best drilled, best shooting and most efficient companies in the Aberdeen infantry volunteers. Indeed, with regard to shooting, some of the students became such expert marksmen that they competed for the King's Prize at Bisley. This was the principal award at the annual National Rifle Association championships, and the championships were open to all members, past and present, of the armed forces.

The success of U Company was largely due to its first captain, the redoubtable W O Duncan, who was then a partner in the Aberdeen legal firm of Peterkin and Duncan. In group photographs of U Company he is a striking figure with a large moustache and looks every inch a soldier. His claymore with

Colonel Douglass Duncan

its scabbard has a place of honour today in the headquarters of the University Officers Training Corps in Old Aberdeen. Duncan was an excellent judge of men, and his unconventional methods and attention to detail were responsible for some unusual features – to be described – in the training of a body of part-time student soldiers.

Renewed Interest in Volunteering

By the beginning of 1897 the enthusiasm for volunteer soldiering at the University had largely died out, and the Heavy Battery had great difficulty in attracting new recruits. Captain Duncan held strong views on the reasons for the lack of success of the University Artillery unit and felt that it was due to two factors. The first was that there had been too close a connection with the professorial staff of the University, and the second factor – and more important in Duncan's mind – was

Captain W O Duncan

that for too many years the same student had continued as the Battery's Sergeant-Major. This led Duncan to introduce changes both in attendance at drills and shooting, and in the way that promotions were handled in a military unit. Special arrangements were made to suit the peculiar circumstances of the students, and the regulation number of drills was reduced so that there would be the minimum interference with their studies.

The most unusual new feature that Duncan introduced into the running of U Company was the imposition of a strict limit on the period of office of the colour-sergeant and sergeants. Sergeants automatically reverted to the rank of private at the end of each academic year to allow for fresh promotions. The ladder of promotion was not blocked and students climbed up and moved on. By the end of 1913 there was a roll of 14 ex-colour-sergeants and 56 sergeants – all fully trained and efficient men turned out by one small unit. At the outbreak of the war in 1914 many of these ex-sergeants, and a number of ex-colour sergeants, who had graduated from the University, were serving as private soldiers in U Company. Duncan's drive, and single-mindedness, was responsible for a great upsurge in volunteering, and at the turn of the century some 260 students were enrolled with U Company and the medical unit. This represented more than a third of the male students – a greater number than were involved in the numerous University sporting activities open to students.

W O Duncan (*centre left*) with his successor Captain Edward Watt (*centre right*)

Duncan was succeeded in 1906 by Captain Edward W Watt, MA, a former editor of *Alma Mater* and a future Lord Provost of Aberdeen, under whose captaincy U Company, in July of 1906, made their famous route march of over 70 miles from the Battalion's annual camp at Barry, near Carnoustie, back home to Aberdeen. In 1908, during Watt's captaincy, the 1st Volunteer Battalion became the 4th Battalion of the Gordon Highlanders and in the same year, like all other volunteer establishments, the Battalion was brought into the Territorial Force scheme. This scheme was created by the Minister for War, Richard Burdon Haldane, the first Viscount Haldane and himself a Scotsman, who was also responsible for introducing Officers Training Corps. The introduction of the Territorial Force and an OTC scheme was to prove a critical time for U Company. The student soldiers had a choice between joining a corps which would guarantee them a commission in the event of war or carrying on as privates and non-commissioned officers in the 4th Gordons. The entire Company elected to continue on the old lines, and who will say that they were wrong?

W O Duncan retired as the Lieut-Colonel commanding the 4th Battalion of the Gordon Highlanders in 1913 after 26 years service with the unit, and by that

Private John Kirton as a colour-sergeant

time the commanding officer of U Company was another lawyer, Captain Lachlan Mackinnon, a member of a well-known Aberdeen family of advocates. 'Lachie' Mackinnon had himself come up through the ranks of U Company and was on record as saying that it was much more fun being a private in the Company than being its captain. The total number of students enrolled in U Company during the 17 years from its beginning in 1897 up to the outbreak of the Great War in 1914 was close on 600, and almost three-quarters of that number were students and graduates of the Faculty of Arts. At the beginning of the war on 4 August 1914 the official strength of U Company was 132 men and many of them were graduates in arts and science. One private, John Kirton, MA, MB ChB, – who had entered the university as fifth bursar in 1908 and had been the Colour-Sergeant of U Company in February 1913 – was a graduate in both arts and medicine. The fact that he was a doctor seems to have been overlooked for some time while he was mobilised and trained with U Company, and he was not commissioned into the RAMC until February of 1915.

The Student Soldiers

More than 90 years ago, long before the first war, peace-time soldiering with the Aberdeen University Company was a very popular and rewarding experience for many students – not unlike being a member of the football, shinty or rugby teams except that one volunteered to join rather than being chosen. There was also the small matter of pay. Students in those days were as impecunious as they are now, and *Alma Mater* was able to announce in October 1913 that the Company meeting would be held on the 24th at Marischal College when arrears of pay would be distributed and promotions announced. It was hoped that every man would bring along his younger comrades to sign on as members of the best organisation in the Varsity. A keen first or second-year student recruit, particularly one who excelled at some sporting activity, had every chance of promotion to the rank of non-commissioned officer. One man held the highest rank of Colour-Sergeant – signalled by the wearing of a golden crown on the sleeve of his tunic – and the holder was regarded by new students with the same respect as the President of the Students Union or the President of the Students' Representative Council. When U Company was mobilised in 1914, the Colour-Sergeant was James D Pratt, a graduate of 1913 and an assistant lecturer in Chemistry at the University, whose MA and BSc were both honours degrees. All the sergeants were graduates and some had honours degrees, and many of the rank and file were graduates with teaching or other jobs. They gave up these posts to rejoin the Company of their student days in August of 1914.

One of the attractions of belonging to U Company was the opportunity for wearing the kilt and the striking sporran which were provided free with the rest of the uniform. In those days of predominantly dark and somewhat drab clothes the student soldiers would have cut quite a dash – particularly in female eyes – and even more so at their annual ball at the University in the spring term where they and their partners danced the lancers, reels and the highland schottische, attired as they were in full dress uniform with white spats, red flashes at their hose tops, Gordon tartan kilts, red tunics and large tartan plaids. This uniform was also worn on ceremonial occasions such as the parade held on the links at the Aberdeen sea front on 29 August 1913 when Field Marshal Lord Roberts presented new colours to the 4th Battalion of the Gordon Highlanders in front of 30,000 spectators. Lord Roberts, a tiny man, was quite dwarfed beside Captain Lachlan Mackinnon, the commander of U Company, who was over six feet in height and wore a tall feathered head-dress.

The Colours presented by Lord Roberts

The students probably looked rather less glamorous in their khaki tunics on company route marches through and around Aberdeen, or on church parades to the lovely old University chapel at King's College in Old Aberdeen; but the appeal of the kilt worn by a body of fit and healthy young men on the march was always present. Another important feature was the lasting appeal of the bagpipe and drum bands of the Highland battalions for Scottish men and women, with the vigorous reveille of *Hey Johnnie Cope, are ye waukin' yet*, or the haunting tune, often played at funerals, *The Flowers O' the Forest Are a' Wede Awa*.

Yet another attraction for the members of U Company was two weeks' paid holiday at the annual summer camp which, on 18 July 1914, was again held in glorious weather at Tain in Ross-shire on the shores of the Dornoch Firth. There the

Bathing parade on the beach at Tain

students threw off the cares and anxieties of recent degree examinations with some rigorous military training accompanied by a good deal of student devilment, – some of the student soldiers rowed across the Firth to Dornoch 'to give the girls a treat' – and amused themselves and the locals with their large repertoire of choruses from various sources including the *Students' Song Book*. Parades commonly finished at half past three in the afternoon and in the long northern summer evenings there was plenty of time for swimming in the sea or playing golf on the excellent Tain links course. In the second week there was a Battalion football tournament, usually won by U Company, a golf match against the members of Tain Golf Club, a Battalion sports meeting and a field-firing shooting competition. The end of the second week of the annual camp was celebrated by a huge bonfire around which the volunteer soldiers held a sing-song fuelled by some bottles of beer, but the sudden news on 30 July of impending mobilisation for war with Germany cut short the camp and they promptly headed for home.

A rest during a route march at Tain

11

Outbreak of War

When war was declared the 4th Territorial Battalion of the Gordon Highlanders was mobilised immediately at Aberdeen and with it the University Company which formed roughly about one sixth of the Battalion. U Company, by its diversity, was at that time more representative of Scotland than any other war-time unit of the same size. Although the majority of its members were from Aberdeen and the North-East, students from Caithness and the Lothians served in the ranks with Gaelic speakers from the Hebrides and the Western Isles.

Among those mobilised with the 4th Gordons was the young Eric Linklater who was still at the Grammar School in Aberdeen and who had managed to enlist five months previously, immediately after his 15th birthday. Linklater, as usual, stood out in a crowd, – in later life he was known in artistic circles in Edinburgh for his 'crumpled elegance' – but on this occasion for all the wrong reasons. The narrow-shouldered, short-sighted and bespectacled boy with his brand new kilt and khaki tunic rather too large for him, was soon spotted and was ignominiously discharged as unfit. Nothing daunted, he tried again a year later and with the help of Captain James Stewart of the RAMC he managed to get himself passed fit for army service as he recounted in his lively memoir, *Fanfare For A Tin Hat*, published in 1970. Jimmy Stewart was an Aberdeen doctor who saw some severe fighting in France in the early months of the war and was then posted to garrison duty at Castlehill Barracks in Aberdeen. There he had incurred the wrath of the

Provost Marshal for walking outside barracks without gloves, but his chief crime was to be seen smoking a pipe while walking down Union Street in uniform. As a result of this Stewart had lost patience with authority and he decided to assist the young Linklater with his schemes. He was told to present himself at Castlehill Barracks at eight o'clock in the morning, before any senior officers had arrived, and he was soon declared fit for home service by Captain Stewart who then called him a damned fool for wanting to join the infantry.

As an Orderly Corporal in the Fife and Forfar Yeomanry, Linklater managed

12

to adjust his medical record by improving the quality of his eyesight and adding a year to his age, and then signed the detail sending himself and a draft of the Black Watch to France. There he saw action at Passchendaele and suffered a very serious head wound in the German advance of March 1918. He survived to become a medical student – although he later graduated in arts – at the University of Aberdeen after the war, and in 1924 he became a sergeant in the re-formed University Company of the 4th Gordons. In 1920 Linklater helped to inaugurate the first student Gala Week, whose chief purpose was to raise money for the local hospitals, and for a number of years he wrote the libretto for the week-long revue staged in His Majesty's Theatre during Gala Week. His first job after graduating was as a leader writer for, and assistant editor of, *The Times of India* in Bombay.

Before it embarked for France in February of 1915, U Company officially became D Company, but old traditions die hard and it continued to be referred to unofficially as U Company by its members. Scottish infantry battalions at the outset of the war in 1914 consisted of eight companies lettered from A to H, but by January 1915 they were reorganised into four double companies A, B, C and D. U Company was in truth D Company although this did not become effective – for reasons which will become obvious – in the eyes of either the Company or the Battalion until October of 1915. And so the name U Company, originally given to distinguish it as a University unit, officially lapsed in 1915. But in regimental annals names hallowed by tradition tend to persist, despite the edicts of Whitehall. The 75th and 92nd Regiments of Foot had never lost their old identities, though amalgamated in 1881 to form the 1st and 2nd battalions of the Gordon Highlanders. General Sir Ian Hamilton, himself an old Gordon, has recorded how in that year an effigy of the 'Ninety-Second' was buried with funeral pomp on the green slopes of a South African mountain. During the night some unknown hero braved the wrath of Lord Wolseley and the War Office by setting up a tombstone over the grave, bearing on it the words –

Ninety Twa, no deid yet.

In the words of Alexander Rule (a member of U Company): – 'such a precedent serves to justify the retention of the original title of a University Unit which, even after months of heavy trench warfare in the Ypres salient, sang *Gaudeamus* to the end'.

On mobilisation, most, although not all, members of U Company immediately set off with the 4th Battalion of the Gordon Highlanders for a few days at Perth on the way to their training ground at Bedford. There they were to be worked hard to get fit before they were sent to France. If the martial zeal of the Germans was missing, it was felt that they could at least be matched in physical efficiency, although this was soon to prove a poor substitute for the large discrepancy between the Germans and the British in the number of machine guns per battalion. When U Company embarked at Southampton in February of 1915 for their eventual destination in Flanders the strength of the Company was about 130 men. They can have had little idea of what lay ahead of them.

Aberdeen before the Great War

What sort of life did these young men leave in Aberdeen when they set off for a war which was to wipe out the brightest and best of a whole generation? A great deal depended on their station in life, and although their backgrounds might differ

– students were among the more privileged – some things were common to all. The city's churches were packed with worshippers on a Sunday and young men and women not uncommonly attended all three services. The morning service was held from eleven until after twelve, then Sunday school as a pupil or teacher at three o'clock followed by the evening service from six until seven. Over 80 years ago the great majority of University students in Aberdeen belonged to the town, although there were student 'digs' for increasing numbers from the country and from the Western Isles. Rosemount was the favoured area and many landladies had been mothering and looking after their student charges for a long number of years. Dr James Fraser, himself a member of U Company as a student and who was a well-known general medical practitioner in Aberdeen for many years, recalled in his memoirs, *Dr Jimmy*, published by his family after his death in 1979, that in his time student lodging was confined to practically two areas of Aberdeen, the Rosemount district and Kittybrewster, which was becoming popular with arts students because of its proximity to King's College. He particularly remembered how a student walking down Rosemount and whistling the first few bars of *Gaudeamus* or *Ho Ro My Nut Brown Maiden* would cause windows to be thrown open to discover who was there. There were far fewer students than today: less than one per cent of the population went to university, and men greatly outnumbered women.

Motor cars were rare in the Aberdeen of the pre-war years, but even the well-to-do walked to church on Sundays and journeys of a mile or more were common. Most Aberdonians had never seen an aeroplane, and as the population was largely immobile, many had travelled little outside the city boundaries. Bicycles were not uncommon but the normal daily method of transport was the tram car, first horse-drawn and then electrical. In common with many other things, tram cars did not run on the Sabbath which was regarded everywhere as a day of rest. Sunday sport was unheard of and even boating on the river Dee was frowned upon. In many households a pack of playing cards could not be produced although simpler games were permitted, particularly where children were involved. The more affluent Aberdonians lived in the west end or the outskirts of the city in detached or semi-detached houses made of granite which was quarried locally at Rubislaw. Most of Aberdeen was built of this clean, bright stone and as a result it was a more handsome city than the other principal Scottish towns, but it was not without its quota of small and very unpleasant slums. It was widely described as the granite city, and sometimes as 'the silver city by the sea', and its citizens knew that Aberdeen granite was famous the world over. Tales were told of the magnificent, if somewhat bizarre, Victoria railway terminus in Bombay, constructed in the 19th century, which had roofs supported by columns made from granite brought from Aberdeen. In 1914 the majority of houses were lit by gas using incandescent mantles, and the gas lamps which illuminated the streets were lit each evening by the familiar figure of the lamplighter – known to generations of Scottish children as the leerie – as he made his rounds with his long pole over his shoulder.

In the countryside outside Aberdeen, before the war, about one in four of the working population was employed in agriculture, but in the town the principal service industry of the time was domestic service, with about 15 per cent of the population employed in this way. Local and national newspapers carried regular advertisements from Servants Registry Offices of the posts and the annual wages that could be expected - Housemaid £18, Cook-General £24, House-Parlour Maid £22, Scullery Maid £14, Third Housemaid £18 and Generals £20 and £24 were among many examples of the work on offer. Others on the Register were Companion Helps, Mother's Helps, Working-Housekeepers, Cook-Housekeepers, Children's Maids, Under-Maids, Daily Maids and Charwomen.

Health

Provision for the sick in Aberdeen before the Great War was far removed from the National Health Service as we know it today. Among the commonest diseases were pneumonia, tuberculosis, poliomyelitis, the venereal diseases of gonorrhoea and syphilis, and the serious diseases of childhood such as measles, whooping cough, scarlet fever and diphtheria which were a frequent cause of death not only in children but also in adults. The vaccines and antibiotics which would radically reduce the incidence and improve the treatment of these conditions were undreamt of in these days. The scourge of tuberculosis claimed the lives of many young people, and over 80 years ago some three and a half thousand died annually from the disease compared with 30 such deaths per annum in the present day. The risk of infection from other diseases was considerable and in 1905 there was an epidemic of typhus in Aberdeen, while nearby Peterhead in 1907 had almost 300 cases of typhoid fever.

The parish hospital of Oldmill (now Woodend Hospital) was the resting place of the poor while the less poor were treated free of charge in the so-called 'voluntary' hospitals. The voluntary hospital system was funded by contributions from the general public, and this was commonly the biggest local charity in the city and the surrounding area. In the 19th and 20th centuries the Aberdeen Royal Infirmary received its subscriptions from a large number of sources: in the work place and from friendly societies, donations from patients and their relatives who had been treated without payment, the income from numerous legacies and investments and the annual 'Hospital Sunday' church collections. Door-to-door collections were held in the country but not in the city, and after the war all the money raised by the University students during their annual gala week was given to the Infirmary.

All patients were treated by the honorary (unpaid) medical and surgical staff of the hospitals free of charge and the staff supported themselves entirely by their private practices. The first annual church collection for the Infirmary in Aberdeen was instituted by an Act of Synod which was printed and sent out to the clergy in April 1748 and collections continued for 200 years until the last appeal on 11 January 1948. This was a relic of the early days of Christian civilisation in Europe when care of the sick was regarded as a religious duty and the erection of hospitals was considered a worthy enterprise of the church.

Entertainment

The young people of today, accustomed as they are to a continuous diet of radio and television programmes, must wonder how their forebears entertained themselves more than 80 years ago. There were no wireless sets as the first entertainment broadcasting did not take place until 1922. Even then the reception was confined to enthusiasts who, before the days of valves, could be bothered with manipulating a 'cat's whisker' to receive an uncertain and irregular signal, frequently masked by atmospherics. The focal point of many homes was the upright piano around which family and friends would gather in the evenings and sing the popular songs of the times. The popular music of these days was divided into a number of categories such as religious (hymns and psalms), military (*My Old Shako*), poetry set to music as in Rudyard Kipling's *On The Road to Mandalay*, music for dancing, and sentimental songs.

The cinema was another form of entertainment which played an increasingly prominent part in everyday life. The silent moving films made by Mack Sennet and featuring the marvellously incompetent Keystone Cops, and later Charlie Chaplin, filled the 'picture palaces' of the Electric Cinema, the La Scala Theatre and the Picture House, and were regarded with wonder as well as providing great amusement

15

for young and old alike. His Majesty's Theatre played to full houses with such shows as *The Merry Widow,* and most young people would have attended the circus and perhaps even have seen the famous Buffalo Bill's Wild West Show which toured Britain in the early years of the century.

John Forbes Knowles

John Knowles was fairly typical of the young men of his class who grew up in Aberdeen before the Great War and were to become members of U Company. He was born in the city on 26 February 1891. His parents were not well-to-do, but, in the best traditions of the North-East of Scotland, they were determined to make sacrifices so that he could have a university education. He was educated at the Grammar School in Aberdeen and then at the University of Aberdeen where he graduated Master of Arts in 1912. He then entered the United Free Church College to pursue his studies in divinity and he continued to study for the ministry of the Church of Scotland both in Aberdeen and Edinburgh until the outbreak of war. It was said of him that his exceptional gifts as an elocutionist, combined with his scholarship, pointed to a distinguished career as a preacher. The UFC College students carried out work in the east end of Aberdeen known as the 'Spital Mission' and Knowles played an active and enthusiastic part in it. Although his health was far from robust, in October 1914 he rejoined U Company of the 4th Gordons in which he had served as a volunteer in his student days.

Knowles was popular with his fellow students and was described as having a genial and sunny temperament, but with a determined approach to life. He was known by his friends as a quiet and thorough young man, always 'game', so typical of many in the north-east corner of Scotland. The creed by which his generation lived encouraged many of its young men to devote their lives to the church, and the few remaining records of U Company show that of its members and former members, 17 so-called 'fighting parsons' were killed in action as infantrymen. The question of whether ministers of religion should join the army as fighting men was argued at great length in English newspapers, but it seemed to present no difficulties in Scotland, certainly in the early stages of the war, where parsons joined the ranks of the infantry in considerable numbers. Four of these fighting parsons, all graduates and all in

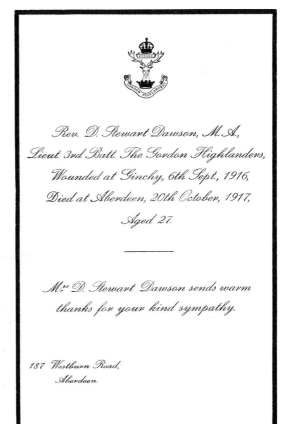

Rev. D. Stewart Dawson, M.A.,
Lieut. 3rd Batt. The Gordon Highlanders,
Wounded at Ginchy, 6th Sept, 1916,
Died at Aberdeen, 20th October, 1917,
Aged 27.

————

Mrs D. Stewart Dawson sends warm
thanks for your kind sympathy.

187 Westburn Road,
Aberdeen.

One of the fighting parsons

the ranks, died defending Ypres with U Company. As with many other young men of the time Knowles was keen on self-improvement, and with a group of friends who all lived in the Mile End area of Aberdeen, he started 'The Corner Club' in 1911. His closest friend was John McConachie who was elected president of the club with Knowles as the vice-president and there were altogether ten members. Associations such as this were not an unusual feature of life in those days and in rural areas Mutual Improvement Societies were very common.

THE CORNER CLUB 1911

| | J A McConachie | | Chas Stephen | | Jas Walker | |
| L Davie | | E S Connon | | J F Knowles | | Lewis D Matthews |

Meetings of the Corner Club were held on Saturday nights in the homes of the members in rotation, and the surviving minute book for 1912 and 1913 suggests that they were lively and jolly affairs. The objects of the club were to discuss subjects of interest and other matters and to hear papers read by members on subjects familiar to them. Knowles led off with one on 'Physical Culture', and this was followed on successive Saturdays by talks on 'The Boer War and how we muddled through', 'Religion', 'Electrical and Mechanical Engineering', 'Military training in the Territorials', 'Has society any claim on our lives?', 'Will Aberdeen win the Scottish Cup?', 'Home Rule for Ireland' and 'Canada, the land of the future', among many others. On two successive years the club held their annual 'At Home' at different venues with their lady friends at which they sang solos, had supper and danced until two in the morning – but on a weekday.

It was not uncommon for young men in those pre-war days to keep diaries and Knowles was no exception. The only remaining written words of his are contained in his diary for 1914-1915 and it serves as a daily record of the University Company as seen through his eyes. He was 23 years of age when he went to war.

CHAPTER TWO

The Diary of Private John F Knowles MA

4th November 1914. We left Aberdeen for Bedford a body of 320 men of the 4th Battalion Gordon Highlanders, entraining at Aberdeen at 6.30 p.m.. [This was a draft to bring the Battalion up to strength]. We had been finally mobilised at 2.30 p.m. and were not permitted to leave headquarters at Woolmanhill till we were ready to move off. It was just on Wednesday, the day before, that we were thunderstruck when Lt-Colonel [J E] McQueen, Officer Commanding the 4th Reserve Battalion Gordon Highlanders, announced that we were to depart for Bedford on the following day. I had not been prepared for this, and though like many others I cheered at the announcement, also, I am sure like many others, the cheer proceeded from a heart whose real feelings might have better been expressed by a groan. It was not that I was not eager to get into the thick of it as soon as possible, but I had not expected to leave home for a few weeks at least. I was eager to get away, but wished for some time, a clear day at least, to prepare for departure, to arrange things and to say good-bye. It was not as though I were to return soon - perhaps never. As it was, I rushed my kit together, made my Will leaving my goods to my mother and sister Jessie, and got ready to go at the time commanded.

We had a sorry march down to the Joint station, the rain pouring down and the streets thronged with people, who pressed forward so eagerly to speak and shake hands with those they recognised, that our lines were soon broken and men falling out to speak to friends made us a ragged column of march. The darkness also added to the confusion, the town being in darkness owing to the aeroplane scare, so that by the time we got into Guild Street we had to shoulder our way through the crowd. Women were shrieking and weeping, whether because of losing their husbands and sweethearts or because of the pressure of the crowd it was well nigh impossible to determine.

I managed to get into a carriage with five University men I knew, and we made ourselves comfortable. The journey was quite an experience. Never for a moment was there perfect quiet. In many of the carriages there was not a man sober, and drunks were continually perambulating the corridor, while the special police and NCOs were following them up and trying in vain to preserve order. At Edinburgh station several men managed to get out of the train, though we were not permitted to do so. One man, in trying to get out of the window, fell and smashed his head. He was a very wild-looking character, and when his eye was bandaged up he looked worse than ever. Another drunk paid frequent visits to our carriage, and interviewed us through the window of the corridor door. He was quite amiable at first, but finally wanted to fight us all. In one of his visits, as we would not allow him to open the door, he leaned over and put his fist through the inside glass, cutting his hand fearfully. At this we got up and opened the door, ordering him to clear out. This he did readily enough, as the falling glass appeared to have cowed him somewhat. The same individual had a most raucous voice, with which he kept singing all the time some air about 'a hielan' melody'.

How difficult it is to rest in a full railway carriage. The six of us took off our boots and placed our feet on the seat opposite. At first it seemed the acme of comfort, but it becomes painful after several hours to support the legs by the feet alone. Nevertheless I managed to snatch an hour or two of uneasy slumber. At Carlisle we got some lemonade at an exorbitant figure.

Weary and worn we arrived at Bedford at 9.30 a.m. on a cold morning, and were marched up to headquarters at Lansdowne Road to the regimental march of 'Hielan' Laddie' played by the Battalion pipe band. The Drum Major (Wilson, a butcher in South Mount Street, Aberdeen) is a very funny man. He stands before the band as if he were the Commanding Officer, and when there is a halt, he poses in stage attitudes, which gives rise to much laughter.

We had breakfast in a mud pond (back garden) behind 12, Lansdowne Road. Then twelve of us were billeted in No. 3 in three attic rooms absolutely destitute of furniture. There were small mattresses on the floor for beds and that was all the furnishings.

7th Dec. We have been shifted from 3 Lansdowne Road to No. 5 Conduit Road. It is an empty house and those of us who were at No. 3 occupy the ground floor. There are two rooms and kitchen and scullery. I am in charge of the back room being senior man, and there are two recruits and another man, making four of us in all. It is a very pleasant room with a French Window, and looks quite habitable though we have to sleep on the floor. We get on very well together in the room, and so far there has been no trouble about division of labour.

Tuesday 8th Dec. I was inoculated for Typhoid at 4.15 p.m. after the day's parade. The operation consists of an injection of germs into the upper arm and is not very painful. I felt my arm slightly sore after, but this was chiefly due to the friction of my clothes. Otherwise I felt much as usual in spite of the 'germ' struggle that must have been going on inside. We were allowed three days sick parade, as it is very dangerous to catch a cold after being inoculated. (N.B. Inoculation is quite different from vaccination). The second inoculation is not supposed to be done till at least ten days after the first, and only two days sick parade is allowed.

A soldier's life appears to me to be very monotonous and makes a man a machine. This is what I actually feel, for I do not feel inclined much for reading, and newspapers I seldom see, though I could get any amount. War news or any news possess little attraction for me. The more efficient I am becoming as a soldier, the less is my intellect developing. The conclusion I arrive at from this is that military training only makes a man superficially intelligent. The most important part of his being is left slumbering. It is alertness and not intelligence that is demanded from a soldier. We have to do things which I can see no reason for, nor is there any reason given.

In our last billet we got a good laugh at Lt Hopkinson who is a very good sort though not particularly efficient. He came into our billet at No. 3 Lansdowne Road to inspect us and he said that our beds were nicely arranged but that there was to be a 'consultation of officers' to see how it would be best to arrange the beds and blankets. In this little incident we have focused the actual standard of efficiency to which our officers have attained. 'Internal economy' is their favourite order when we have any spare time. This is all very well, but it is difficult to follow a man as a leader who is no better than a sanitary inspector, and yet pays attention to useless trifles.

So long as you shave regularly and clean your buttons, rifle, spats, cap etc., your skin and underclothing may be as dirty as you please. Of course this is all very well again, but we expect a man to have a soul above clean buttons. Captain Mackinnon is worst of all the officers to please. Durward truly described him as a 'fed-up hairpin'. He is over six feet in height, round backed, narrow shouldered and altogether ridiculous as he peers at a man to see if he is properly dressed.

Captain Lachlan Mackinnon

20

Tribulations of life in the Army

The Lachlan Mackinnon, MA, BL, LLB, mentioned above, followed in his father's footsteps by enlisting in the 1st Volunteer Battalion of the Gordon Highlanders in 1903 and was commissioned in 1905. He was a Captain in the 4th Gordons and the officer commanding U Company when he was mobilised on 4 August 1914. He then had a very distinguished career as a civilian soldier and he was awarded the DSO and Croix de Guerre in France and reached the rank of Lieut-Colonel. Knowles and his student friend James Durward must have been upset badly by their company commander over something as this entry in the diary is somewhat out of character. James Durward served in France continuously for four years. He was commissioned in 1917, twice mentioned in despatches, and finished the war as a captain himself. Like other student veterans of the Great War he was mature beyond his years when he returned to his studies and he graduated MA with first class honours in mathematics in 1919.

That military discipline should prove a problem in U Company was hardly surprising as officers, NCOs and men all knew one another so well and many graduates who were long past boyhood were serving in the ranks. The officers had all come through the ranks of U Company, and as has already been seen, students who had reached the rank of sergeant after a number of years of service, reverted to the rank of private at the beginning of each new University year. The Company Sergeant-Major, J D Pratt, was an assistant lecturer in chemistry at the University and with his two first-class honours degrees was better qualified academically than many of his officers. Like other members before mobilisation, he had been accustomed to call Captain Mackinnon – a conscientious man not famed for his sense of humour – 'Lachie', when not on parade, and this was an obstacle to the serious business of preparing for war. This matter was aired after the war by General Sir Richard Bannatine-Allason who commanded the 51st Highland Division from August 1914 until September 1915. His remarks demonstrated how the British, in comparison with the peoples of the continent of Europe, were anything but a martial race at the outset of the Great War.

It must be remembered that Britain was alone among the great powers in not having a system of compulsory military service before the war, whereas in France, for example, compulsory military service had been increased from two to three years in 1913; and in common with Russia and Germany a substantial part of the French budget was being spent on the army. In Bewsher's *History of the 51st Highland Division*, published in 1921, Bannatine-Allason stated that it was originally laid down that Territorial troops would require six months for complete training. He noted that most of the equipment available at the outbreak of war such as guns, rifles and technical stores was quite out of date and also ridiculously inadequate. In addition, most of the permanent staff of Territorial battalions such as adjutants and NCOs, who were regular soldiers, had been sent elsewhere on more important duties. Discipline in barracks was excellent but field discipline left much to be desired. It was sometime before some Commanding Officers could be made to understand that an order in the field did not admit of heated argument before execution – and the rank and file had to learn that training was not a recreation to stop when they felt tired. This took a little time to be appreciated but in a matter of months units began to assume a workmanlike and serviceable appearance on parade.

Alma Mater

Many members of U Company had been active in the corporate and social life of the University and had been contributors to *Alma Mater*. One of their number,

Private John (Jack) H S Mason who graduated MA with honours in English in 1911, had been the editor of *Alma* in 1911-12. The magazine continued to publish articles and letters from the Company while it was training in Bedford and on active service in France and Belgium. One of the earliest contributions in October 1914, from the pen of Jack Mason, was on the vexed subject of discipline and it was published under the heading – 'Patriots All'.

Jack Mason

The first serious if temporary obstacle to our comfort was the sudden tightening of the strings of discipline. It was a little difficult for us to learn implicit obedience to our yesterday's equal in civil life. Even in camp [in peacetime], the training was a sort of episode in the communal enjoyment of life under canvas. Conviviality and camaraderie were the essence of the fortnight's discipline. Here, it dawned on us with disconcerting suddenness that drill and training had become our *raison d'être*. The discovery revealed the adaptability of human nature, and was good for us privates; the NCOs took some time to accustom themselves to their power, and even now have some difficulty in striking the happy medium. However, like other phenomena, they have to be accepted philosophically. We have managed to become 'swaddies' in necessary points, while retaining our student life socially. We have not been reduced to a Gissingese distaste of being mere numbers, except in rare moments. The advance party in Perth created a favourable impression for the Battalion with an impromptu concert - 'R Reid and flute *ducentibus*'. [Robert Reid MA, was commissioned into the 9th Battalion of the Gordons after three months training with U Company at Bedford. He was killed in May 1916].

Alma Mater arrived in Bedford on Thursday afternoons and was awaited eagerly as the one remaining strong link with university life. Articles submitted by the student soldiers continued to appear, and in the month of November '*U Company Notes*' reported that MacLennan had the honour of supplying the first good joke since mobilisation. He had delivered a new 'Grace' - 'For what we are about to receive; Lord give us sufficient vocabulary'. The notes concluded:

Discipline is a matter of small things, and it is perhaps because of this that students do not take kindly to it. It is so natural to remember days when to be late at classes was a distinction, and when untidy digs were no stigma. But classes are not parades, nor digs billets. Pack drill may await any who fail to make the distinction. Spats, cap-badges and buttons must be without spot, for these (who can doubt) are the things that will eventually defeat the Germans.

Founded in 1883, *Alma Mater* was an outstanding and widely read magazine during the almost 80 years of its existence. The masthead for many years depicted a student in gown and mortar board leaning on the crown at King's, while on the other side the sporting interests of the students were illustrated by a tasselled cap, a rugby ball and a rifle - also leaning on the crown.

John Keith Forbes

John Knowles, writing in his diary, was far from alone in his criticism of what he saw as petty military discipline and the unquestioning obedience of any order. Another fighting parson in U Company who could think for himself was his divinity student friend, the legendary John Keith Forbes, immortalised in the short biography entitled *Student and Sniper-Sergeant* and published in 1916 after his death in action at Hooge in September 1915. J K Forbes was born in Aberdeen in 1883 and graduated Master of Arts at the University in 1905, and for the next seven years taught at Rathven School near Buckie. He came from a remarkable family which had a distinguished academic record both on his mother's side and his father's. One of his uncles, Sir Arthur Keith, was an Aberdeen graduate who later became Hunterian professor at the Royal College of Surgeons in England.

Forbes developed a passion for music and taught himself to play a number of musical instruments, and in 1908 he was appointed organist and choir-master to Buckie parish church. As a member of the Banff orchestral society as a cellist in 1910 he was accustomed to cycle from Buckie to Banff and back again on the same night, a distance of 40 miles, with his cello strapped to his back. He was also a hill-walker and climber of note. One of his contemporaries wrote of him that his 'character was cloaked by certain eccentricities', but these seemed to be nothing more than a liking for solitude and such 'utter lack of care for his personal appearance' that on one occasion at least he was taken for a tramp. Forbes was known to walk over moors and unfrequented roads for 30 miles at a stretch; often walking by night guided by the stars. A very keen golfer, he would spend a whole day on the golf course at Spey Bay practising with one particular club and a dozen balls. He was fluent in Doric and frequently spoke it, which may have struck others as odd in an educated man. Having satisfied himself that teaching was not fulfilling enough, he decided to enter the church and enrolled in the United Free Church College in Aberdeen in 1912.

The colleges of the United Free Church were well known for their high level of scholarship, but J K Forbes was an outstanding student. He had never studied Greek until the summer he left Rathven, but a few months of study was all that he required to master it. He left college one Easter with the intention of studying German, and when he returned in October he was reading *Goethe* and *Eucken* in the original with ease. He took the first place in the examinations open to all the colleges in Scotland, in addition to winning the Foote scholarship in Hebrew and the Eadie prize in New Testament Greek. Having already been a member of U Company, he enlisted in October 1914 as a private in the 4th Gordons. He could probably have obtained a commission but was content with the rank of sergeant, believing as he did that as an NCO he would be able to exercise a greater moral influence on his men. He always carried with him the Book of Job in the Hebrew original, and even in the trenches he found time to translate it and make notes on the text, using a commentary in German and a German dictionary.

John Keith Forbes

J K Forbes was a very unusual man with high ideals. When he arrived in Bedford he was put into U Company and expressed his displeasure in his first letter home. He wrote that the Company was first-class but that he had asked for a transfer to another company with a 'rougher' crowd - more of the kind he had been with at Aberdeen. He felt that it was a holiday being among men of his own cast of mind and made it clear that he was not very pleased: among other men he felt he had some real work to do. The 31 year-old Forbes was not enamoured of the period of training at Bedford and in his letters and diary he referred frequently to the stress laid on button cleaning, the abuse of authority and what he saw as the terrible philistinism of the army system. He described kit inspection as a marvel of military life. The blanket had to be a particular length and breadth with the other blankets folded in the approved style on the bed, and on the floor the owner's kit, from cap to bootlaces and oil-bottle to hair brush, arranged in a symmetrical military pattern. He went on to describe the solemn inspection by the sergeant to see that everything was present and correct, followed by the lieutenant to see that the laces were in their proper place, and finally the captain to check that his subordinates had been doing their duty. If it was a field day in the 'Interior Economy' line, then a real, live General would express amazement at private soldiers possessing expensive safety-razors.

Forbes brought to his new role as a soldier the same energy and dedication with which he pursued his studies. He may have seemed a slightly reluctant member of U Company initially, but as sergeant in charge of the sniper section he soon assembled a group of expert shots. In France he was commended by the General commanding the 3rd Division who wrote to him personally about his invaluable services in organising the snipers, and about the accurate information he had gained of the German positions in front of his Battalion. Alexander Rule goes as far as to state that the Germans were aware of J K Forbes as a very definite personality, and in a tribute to the effectiveness of his work as a sniper, had placed a high price on his head. [The University students' house in Rubislaw Terrace in Aberdeen was named Forbes House in memory of J K.]

Training at Bedford

Many of the 4th Gordons were stationed in Bedford with the rest of the Highland Division from 16 August 1914. The principal local weekly newspaper was the *Bedfordshire Times and Independent* and it advertised itself as the county newspaper for 'Beds. Bucks. Cambs. Herts. Hants. and Northants'. On Friday 14 August 1914, it somewhat guardedly told its readers of the arrival of some 18,000 men of the Highland Division.

> We are informed that owing to the movement of troop trains on Sunday 16th and Monday 17th the London and North Western Railway Station will be closed to ordinary traffic on those days. The destination of the trains is a point east of Bedford. This is the first time in the history of this station which must extend for some sixty years that it had been closed for two successive days - or at all.

On the same date it carried an item about the purchase of horses for the Army which reflected the widespread concern among farmers and businessmen.

> No little commotion has been caused in agricultural and commercial circles by the so-called commandeering of horses and vehicles by the military authorities. It is common knowledge that the general run of prices was from £35 to £45, but more for hunters and the better class of shire horse. There has been a considerable raid on hunters, some of which may have cost their owners a hundred guineas or more. This class of horse is required for officers' chargers and some of the stables have almost been depleted.

Robert Reid, Sandy Skinner, Arthur Spark,
Arthur Hawes (with violin) and Robert Donald

Two members
of U Company

Group at
Bedford

In a Bedford billet

Horses were still widely used by officers in infantry battalions and it was estimated that the Highland Division required some four or five thousand horses for all purposes. A hundred polo ponies were sent from India to Britain as a present from the zemindars [land-owners] of Madras. These ponies did not find favour with many units who preferred hunters, but Major-General Bannatine-Allason was quick to accept them, and it was said that the company commanders and the staffs of the Highland Division went to France better mounted than most comparable formations. Many Scottish Territorial officers had little or no experience of riding and some of their antics on horseback were a source of great delight and unconcealed mirth amongst the rank and file. Highlanders were not 'horsey' people and were often uncomfortable with horses and accidents were not uncommon. The commanding officer of the 4th Camerons, Lt-Colonel Ewan Campbell, was thrown from his mount at Bedford and suffered

Not horsey people !

such severe head injuries that he took no further part in the war. The most famous accident of all occurred early in the war when King George V, reviewing his troops in France, suffered injuries to his ribs when thrown from a horse. The horse was General Sir Douglas Haig's own charger which, to his chagrin, he had chosen personally for the King's use because of its reliability.

In supplying an army in 1914 the most important factors were the supply of food for the men, and feed for the large numbers of horses and mules involved in transporting the army and its supplies. It is almost impossible today with our sophisticated transport systems to imagine the lack of motor transport and the slow and cumbersome methods of moving supplies and munitions for the troops, and the unmetalled British, French and Belgian roads along which they had to be moved.

The following week's edition of the *Bedfordshire Times* carried a report of a town meeting which had been held in the Town Hall on the previous Monday night with the Mayor, Harry Browning, in the chair assisted by Charles Stimson, the Town Clerk.

The meeting was called to let the town know of the committees which had been formed for the distress which it was felt would come. They now had a Distress Committee, a Feeding of Children Committee and an Unemployment Committee. There was a discussion as to how people could help and the number of volunteers required. Mr A. Trustam Eve said they had been very proud to welcome into their homes these Scottish Territorials. (Applause). If they were to have troops in Bedford they would just as soon and rather, have them from Scotland than any other place in the British Isles. But they must be gentle with some of them, because he had come across a man that day who had never been away from his parish before, and had never been in a train. (Laughter). And he did not think very much of it either, for it did not come very fast he said, and it took twenty-eight hours to come down from 'Pe-arth'. (Laughter). The speaker could not see what these men had to do with themselves. When they had done their work they had nowhere to go except their bedroom or the streets. He hoped there would be a subcommittee formed to provide recreation. Other speakers concurred and it was suggested that all the religious bodies in the town should lend their Sunday Schools for the purpose of recreation for the soldiers in the evenings.

On the same date under the heading 'Scotch Drops' it was stated that the Scotsmen fully realised that they were a considerable distance from 'hame', and that they seemed to have spent something like 18 hours on the journey from there. Stories about the Scots had already begun to circulate. One of the earliest was of the inevitable postcard being purchased and Private McPherson calling to his chum from the pavement – 'see if they have a *Dundee Post*'. After Burns' night in January 1915 this regular column was renamed 'Highland Division Haggis'. Another story which the newspaper could not resist appeared at a later date 'with apologies to our Scottish visitors'. It concerned the two Jocks who had gone to London for the day. They were seeing the sights of London from the top of a tram when one said to the other, 'See, there's a bonny lass in front, shall we speak to her?' 'Bide a wee', was the reply, 'until she's paid her fare'. But the story that really made people laugh was that about the new English Colonel seeing the Scottish Territorial sentry on guard. 'Who are you?', he said. Sentry – 'Fine Sir, and hoo's yersel?'

The inhabitants of Bedford were pleasantly surprised to find that their forebodings about the effects of the war on the local economy were misplaced. The arrival of the Highlanders when the town was usually half empty resulted in a demand for civilian labour with much overtime to be worked, and a huge increase in demand in all the businesses that might cater for the troops or provide munitions of war. There were some unusual items in short supply such as false teeth and Mr E N Ching the dentist was soon advertising 'Artificial Teeth – Special Charges for the Troops'. Braggins of Harpur Street had become the Military Tailors, and apart from offering 'Officers Bush Khaki Riding Breeches' they were soon advertising 'Soldiers' Comforts – Balaclava Helmets, Woollen Sweaters and Bed Jackets'. The local paper noted that the Scotsmen soon gave the lie to two hoary old traditions. They started more jokes in the first week than an Englishman could think of in 20 years, and they spent their money with a freedom that threatened to empty the shops and the cellars.

The people of Bedford were not long in taking the Highlanders to their hearts and learning to understand the Scottish dialect. On 30 August the editor of the *Bedfordshire Times* produced a potted history of the Gordon Highlanders including the then 13 names of their Victoria Cross holders and where they had won their decorations. He informed his readers that this information had been gleaned from the *Aberdeen Express*. Much mention was made of Corporal Smith who could play charming tunes on a bicycle pump and was greatly in demand at concerts. Sergeant Runcie, who came from Banff, recalled that Bedford people were a bit alarmed when they heard that a kilted army was to be quartered on them. They had visions of all kinds of savages armed with claymores descending on them. One girl asked him if he did not feel the cold at night sleeping out in the Scottish hills with only a plaid to cover him. Another, knowing the house he was billeted in, remarked that the bath in it would be a great surprise to him, he never having seen one before. As the bath had no water laid on and was upstairs so that the hot water had to be carried from the basement to the bath, he thought that was quite a joke.

Alexander Rule

Private Alexander Rule from Huntly was an enthusiastic student member of U Company who was fortunate to survive the battle at Hooge on 25 September 1915 where he was discovered wounded and barely conscious in a dug-out. He recovered from his wounds and came through the war as a captain with a Military Cross. Returning to his studies in Aberdeen, he graduated MA in 1920 and then took a BSc in forestry in 1921 and thereafter spent much of his life in Australia. In 1934, from

Alexander Rule

his war diary, he wrote a light-hearted, cheerful, and very successful account of U Company's adventures called *Students Under Arms* which was published by the University Press in Aberdeen. The book is a vivid and lively narrative and captures completely the atmosphere of 1914-15, but it has no illustrations and appeared at a time of severe economic depression when his fellow Aberdonians were more concerned with making ends meet than with more accounts of the Great War. Rule described eloquently the arrival of the Scots in the Bedford of 1914 and recounted how the Aberdeen students were happy to go along with the image of being some sort of untutored savages from the mountains of Scotland.

During August 1914 the all-kilted Highland Division streamed into Bedford in trainload after trainload, and the skirl of the bagpipes was heard throughout the land. From wild straths and glens we irrupted overnight into a Cowperesque landscape where the sluggish Ouse lazes through flat meadows bounded by thick hedgerows. Age-old churches, with square Saxon towers or graceful spires, dotted the countryside, and around them nestled thatched cottages with white-washed walls. We came, we saw, and we took possession. We found it good.

The quiet old country town was shaken to its foundations. We doubled the population: sheer weight of numbers alone made us a disturbing factor in its civic life. In addition to our infantry, we had no fewer than twelve pipe bands. Bedford had known uninterrupted peace for centuries; it had suffered no invasion since the Danes arrived in their longboats and sacked the place in the stirring days of old. Our invasion was a peaceful penetration – from the military point of view – but we shattered the calm of 700 years.

U Company, in the vanguard of this invasion, found temporary billets in the suburb of Honeyhill, and our first week there almost convinced the residents that we were semi-savages. They stood in their doorways and gaped at us when we danced an eightsome reel in the street to an accompaniment of hoochs and varsity yells. From a nearby taproom honest countrymen emerged, wiping their lips, and came forward uncertainly as if expecting the apparition to disappear at any moment. We revelled in our barbarian role and solemnly assured our hosts that the kilt was our normal civilian garb; we even had the effrontery to tell them that our wild hoochs represented the semi-articulate call of primitive ancestors, and were still used in communicating from one rocky Hielan' crag to another. 'But don't you wear longer kilts in winter'? The question came from a woman spectator and she was promptly enlightened on the point. Our landladies were equally ingenuous; they gravely showed us how to flush a lavatory and how to turn a gas jet out – obviously fearing we might blow it out. But we somehow managed to keep a straight face all through.

The local newspaper mentioned the appreciation of the Bedfordians of the eightsome and foursome reels and other Highland dances of U Company, and the paper entered into the spirit of things by publishing a photograph and caption contributed by the Scots.

The winter season is now in full swing at the Hotel de Empty, Rue de Rothsay, Bedford, where our photograph was taken. The number of guests is very large, and as will be seen, many are enjoying the unrivalled situation (particularly those on the window-sills). The cuisine is well-spoken of, the food being served at separate tables. Every day the visitors take long walks in the picturesque surroundings of the town. The Hotel de Empty is situated in the pleasantest part of the town, within a minute's walk from the 'front', and among the guests there is always plenty of sport. For terms and other particulars apply to the nearest Recruiting Office.

The Khaki Apron

The khaki apron worn over the kilt and sporran was thought to be for protection from the dirt and mud of a very wet winter. *The Bedfordshire Times* was not to be put off with that story and came up with an explanation which must have surprised and alarmed many in the Highland Division.

The khaki apron worn by the kilted Highland regiments is a familiar object now. It must have saved very many lives in the South African War. Before the apron was adopted the sporran made a regular bulls eye for the Boer sharpshooters but this was nullified when the apron was worn. The khaki apron has remained part of the equipment since it was introduced in the Boer War in 1899, without material alteration. On November 5th, 1899, Lt-Colonel W. G. Gostwyck of the 91st Highlanders (Argyll and Sutherland) sent a letter to the *Inverness Courier* suggesting the apron. He also wrote to the Secretary of State for War, Lord Lansdowne, and the apron was speedily adopted. A telegram was sent to the Cape and on November 26th, fifteen days after the recommendation was made, the Black Watch was wearing the apron at Naawport.

The sporran had not always been worn in battle by Highland troops. In his *History of the Gordon Highlanders*, Greenhill Gardyne, writing of Wellington's campaign in Spain in 1812, remarked that inspections in marching order by general officers frequently took place, the men having their blankets and greatcoats neatly rolled and folded, their dress and accoutrements in the best possible order, and wearing their best hose and rosettes. On great occasions they had their purses [sporrans] on, but these they never wore when marching or fighting, being left with the heavy baggage or strapped on the back of the knapsacks.

Knowles' Diary Continues

Friday 18th Dec. 1914 Some men got twelve days leave home. How I envied them.

Saturday 19th Dec. Heavy field day. I walked twenty miles and had nothing to eat from 7.30 a.m. till 4 p.m. This is nothing unusual. Got my hair cut close all over. I look quite like a bald old man.

Sunday 20th Dec. Now I have written this diary up to date. We had a very careful inspection today by Major [G A] Smith. He is not easy to please. We have now a company mess, which enables us to eat our food more like civilised beings. What a sight it would have been for some of the people in Aberdeen to see us at meals. Out in a muddy back yard, a dozen or so round each dixie, some using their hands and others dipping in their not over clean mugs. I have eaten a piece of bread, one side of which was quite dirty and thought nothing about it. After all we eat a lot of dirt without knowing it, so it can make no difference to the digestion when we do.

AS THEY ARE TODAY

4th Gordons Headquarters
at 14 Lansdowne Road

Stagsden

Monday 21st Dec. A heavy rain mixed at one period with sleet prevented us from parading in the morning. It cleared up towards dinner and we fell in at 1.35 and had a ten mile march round by the east of Bedford. It was extremely cold and very good for marching. Returning home there was a beautiful red sunset and it reminded me of the North, especially the sun setting over the Moray Firth. When we got back to Bedford we were lined up on either side of Dynevor Road to witness the punishment of a court martial. It was quite dark except for the street lamps. I could not see the face of the prisoner clearly, but he seemed a matured man - Sergeant Stewart was the name read out in the indictment. He was accused of beating a private with his fists on the ribs and back. Captain Lyon, junior Major, read out the charge and the decision of the court martial, which was reduction to the ranks. The Sergeant Major cut off his stripes, while the Sergeant of Police marched him up and made him eyes right the Colonel as he was marched back. It was not a pleasant scene to have a share in. One cannot help pitying the culprit, though the punishment was just. I am sure most of the men felt as I did, and there would have been a bit of a row had the punishment been for any other offence such as insubordination.

There seems to be a general feeling of dissatisfaction in the Battalion. Part of this is due to the men themselves being unused to discipline and part to the officers of a Territorial battalion being unable to rise to the present crisis. It is a very different thing being an officer for a fortnight at camp and knowing that there is no real work to be done, to being an officer for an indefinite period and not knowing when or how the Battalion may be called on for service. The same applies to the spirit of the men.

Commissions

This feeling of dissatisfaction in the battalion in December 1914 mentioned by Knowles was certainly present in U Company at this time, and it is obvious from some surviving records that it was, in part, related to the vexed question of applying for commissions. The Company by this time was at full strength and Alexander Rule makes it clear that the members felt that it was in every way ready to take its place in any overseas unit. They felt that they were being held back until the battalion as a whole came up to the required standard. At that time there was still a widespread belief that the war would be short-lived, and U Company began to feel that they might miss the action. Rule had more to say.

We chafed bitterly at the delay, and heartily cursed the War Office and everyone remotely connected therewith. Very few [of U Company], so far, had been tempted by offers of commissions, but it became more and more difficult for us to remain fully conscious of the guerdons of service in the company's ranks. Blasphemously fed up, we even went so far as to offer our services in replacing casualties amongst regular units overseas. Luckily for us, we were refused, for we should have thus sacrificed our glorious privilege of serving in 1915 as a student body.

The Commanding Officer of the 4th Gordons at this time was Lieut-Colonel Thomas (Tommy) Ogilvie. He was well aware of the efficiency of U Company which he regarded as the backbone of his battalion, and he felt that if there were to be widespread applications for commissions from its ranks, then his chance of taking his battalion overseas in the immediate future would be lessened. With the unsettling events of the previous month of November fresh in his mind, Colonel Ogilvie had no stomach or desire for another confrontation in December with this remarkable body of very intelligent and highly articulate young men.

Once again the members of U Company were determined to state their case for going abroad forcibly, and to make matters worse they did not seem to be greatly intimidated by threats of military sanctions. The dissatisfaction in U Company resulted in a steady trickle of University men into commissioned ranks during the months of October, November and December. It has to be said, however, that much of the discontent was due to the widespread feeling that the war would be short-lived and might be over by Christmas. Almost all the Company's members were determined to see some action and to do battle with the Germans as soon as possible. One of them wrote of the 'weary months of training at Bedford when we were itching to be out'.

This was the chief reason for the contretemps in the month of November which was set out clearly and succinctly in a letter from a student in U Company. In any other unit the ring leaders would have been court-martialled. James Anderson wrote home to his brother-in-law from the headquarters of the 4th Gordons at 14 Lansdowne Road in Bedford.

James Anderson writes home to his father

......The Company today, George, in fact the Battalion, is happier than it has ever been since mobilisation. Saturday and Sunday proved to be two days for the rank and file – the democracy of the army. How this came about I shall now proceed to show you, not in detail for that would entail pages upon pages, and even then it would be impossible to make it complete. On Saturday night an order came from the War Office asking for recruits for the 6th Gordons and the 4th Seaforths. [These battalions were already serving in France]. Our Captain [Mackinnon] read the order to us as he had to do and then, by various arguments, did all in his power to dissuade us from replying and hoped that the Company would not be split up.

We got till 6 a.m. next morning to decide. Half the Company came forward and with great difficulty 36 out of 70 volunteers got their names down. He bolted with the sheet and refused to take any more, for which I suppose he could be disrated as it was an order from headquarters. He then had a private interview with the men and, almost in tears, begged them to stay on, for, if they didn't it meant the ruination of

32

the Company as he wouldn't get students to fill it up. It was too late to take the men into his confidence now, this they plainly told him, and this they told him plainly – he could say nothing. They were too exasperated with his tyranny and not a man withdrew. He then asked the reasons, and we told him that he treated us like dogs and not rational beings. He was called anything but a gentleman, but he made no reply. The Colour-Sergeant [J D Pratt] was then detailed to see what influence he had, and if the Captain got his character, the Col. Sgt. got it worse.

Colour-Sergeant J D Pratt

Everything that could be raked up was told him bluntly. The double nature of the Sergeants was put to his face, and he couldn't deny it. His own tyranny was shown him with numerous illustrations and the ridiculous promotions were also discussed. I may tell you the latest promotions. The first was the Captain's servant, promoted to lance-corporal. He is a recruit and on very rare occasions parades with the Company, the consequence being that he is absolutely without training. The second was even worse. A recruit, three weeks joined, who had no right to be in the Company, for he is not a student, has been promoted. The reason for his promotion is self-evident as he is a nephew of the last Company Commander.

At tea-time we had to parade before Colonel Ogilvie. He, of course, would not lower his dignity to argue with a Private, but he lectured us for about a quarter of an hour and hoped we would reconsider our decision, and we showed him what we thought of him by refusing to withdraw. Bullying is not the way to handle students, and though his was an earnest appeal, he insulted the men more than anything else. Today he gave the Battalion a lecture, pretty much the same as he gave us – that the Battalion would be in France pretty soon and there was no need to go to any other and thus spoil the efficiency of the 4th Gordons.

Since this has happened, and it is a big slap in the face to the officers, our Captain and NCOs could not have been more decent, but the deed is done now and it is too late to make promises and compromises. It was a grand opportunity for the men to show their grievances and they took full advantage of it. Four corporals have also volunteered. Of course we don't know whether we shall be wanted or not, nor does it really matter. We have opened the eyes of the officers and shown them what confidence we have in them and how deeply we love them. If we are wanted, ten to one I shall be along with Georgie [his cousin in the 6th Gordons], for they will in all probability reinforce Gordons with Gordons and Seaforths with Seaforths. So much for this.

This letter is an indication of how very unusual this unit was and how its members must have had an influence in the Battalion far beyond their numbers. The promotion system introduced into U Company in 1898 by Captain W O Duncan had been in operation right up to the outbreak of the war, and many of the university men (both students and graduates) serving as private soldiers had already held the rank of sergeant. Private R B (Roy) Topping was a good example. He had enlisted in U Company in 1910 as a 16 year-old science student at Aberdeen and three years later had risen to the rank of colour-sergeant, or company sergeant-major – holding the position just prior to J D Pratt. Topping was once more a private in 1914 (he was promoted to corporal in Belgium in May 1915) and must have been as aware of the military niceties of the situation as any of the members of the Company. The officers of the 4th Gordons, fully alive to these circumstances, must have approached the task of officering U Company with some trepidation.

However, the transfer of many members of the Company to more attractive billets in Bedford in December, and the strong rumours that the Battalion would be going overseas before the main body of the Highland Division led to a calmer atmosphere. Perhaps the letting off steam by indicating that they would not be pushed around had a soothing effect on all concerned. There had already been some defections to the officers' messes of other battalions, but by and large U Company remained relatively intact.

Private R B Topping

John Knowles continues his diary

Wednesday Dec. 23rd We had to prepare for an emergency move.

Thursday Dec. 24th Emergency move repeated. We had a three mile march before dark. Christmas eve was very dull. Most of us are wishing we were at home. We have to stand by with a hundred rounds of ammunition per man. Probably the authorities are taking precautions against a Christmas German raid. A bomb has been dropped on Dover and a transport ship sunk. I am more inclined to think all this emergency business has been to keep the men sober. Christmas day is cold and frosty. Everything looks beautiful. We are still told to stand by. What nonsense. At 1.45 those of us who were billeted in empty houses went by invitation for dinner to a cookery school. The lady, Miss Amy Wansley, was exceedingly gracious and shook hands with the whole fifty-three of us as we entered. We had a beautiful dinner of beefsteak, pudding, coffee etc. and got a packet of cigarettes each. We sat till 4 o'clock and had a sing-song. This is the best time I have had since I came to Bedford. For the time I quite forgot that I had left civil life. Cookhouse is now sounding at five o'clock. I hardly feel able for tea.

1st January 1915 It is pouring rain outside. One day is like another here, except that there is no parade. We were busy up to 12.30 – kit and billet inspection. We also had to wash our feet and knees. Last night, Hogmanay (or as I have heard it called here 'mahogany day', the people not being able to pronounce the Scotch guttural), I was at supper in the Conservative Club Hall, St Peter's Street, given by the Bedford Recreation Committee to seven thousand Scotsmen in Bedford. The other seven thousand are to be fed tonight. It was very enjoyable and the fare provided was most excellent considering the large number catered for. I feel literally fed up today after it. The German bombs have stopped our leave. There is little chance of me getting home for a long time yet. The weather is much colder now. On Tuesday we had a few inches of snow, and it was bitterly cold being in the field from 8.40 to 4.30 p.m. with nothing to eat. The hardest part of our training is standing about in the cold. I can well imagine how indifferent one might become to being shot at after a few days of it. Death would be a welcome release.

I was at a second supper tonight, very similar to the other one. It was held in St Peter's Hall. I did not stay to the concert as it was the same as the preceding night.

Hogmanay in Bedford

The local newspaper carried a long account of the Highland Division's Hogmanay suppers and what appeared to be an entirely new festival to the people of Bedford.

The Hogmanay Supper – A Gigantic Festival

New Year's eve was celebrated in Bedford by holding the most tremendous series of supper parties that have ever taken place, or are ever likely to take place again, in this historic locality. The design of the Borough Recreation Committee was to entertain to the supper called Hogmanay, the whole of the Highland Territorial troops billeted in unfurnished houses in Bedford on New Year's Eve, and the rest on New Year's night. There were no fewer than four hundred stewards on duty and three hundred entertainers for the eighteen huts, tents and public halls used to feed seven thousand men on each night, and the cost of the feast was about a thousand pounds. An appeal was made to Scotland for the money, and nearly the whole of it has been forthcoming from Scottish gentlemen, supplemented by local help. At every hall there was a cold refection of various joints, mainly ham and beef, with tea and coffee followed by hot plum pudding and sauce, tea and cakes and mince pies in abundance and the distribution of cigarettes.

The suppers themselves were teetotal functions, and the military took the precaution of issuing an order closing all premises licensed for the sale of intoxicating liquors in Bedford and in the adjoining country parishes at 2.30 p.m. on both Thursday and Friday. Each supper commenced at 6.30 with the National Anthem. There was then a welcome by the chairman, grace was said by the chaplain, at 7.30 the chairman proposed His Majesty the King and the vice-chairman proposed 'Our Scottish Hosts'. The concert and distribution of cigarettes then took place and at 9.15 the proceedings concluded with *Auld Lang Syne* and *God Save the King*.

As the time for supper approached the streets were enlivened by the companies of men marching to the various halls and singing blithely, but they entered the buildings in a respectful and orderly manner. Major-General Bannatine-Allason and his staff visited all the halls in the course of the evening and other distinguished visitors were the Lord Provost of Aberdeen, Mr James Taggart, and William Maxwell, the editor of the *Aberdeen Daily Journal* whose efforts, along with that of Provost William Ramsay of Elgin, had raised most of the money required to provide the suppers. Starting from the Gymnasium, Lansdowne Road, Lord Provost Taggart visited the following places – The Hut, Chaucer Road, St Martin's Hall, the High School, Priory Street School, Modern School Gymnasium, the Corn Exchange, the Conservative Club and the Rink. At each hall the Lord Provost had a rousing reception and the Scotsmen laughed heartily at his many subtle *bon mots*. [One of his *bon mots* was that the military authorities in Bedford had closed the public houses because they had heard that he, the Lord Provost of Aberdeen, was coming.]

Private Blake of the 4th Camerons kindly consented to give a turn in five of the halls and was taken round by motor. Miss Ruby Bower gave some of her admirable recitations at four halls, and the popular vocalist Private Victor Edwards appeared at four. Each man received a packet of Waverley cigarettes largely through the chairmen at various halls. The stewards wore a badge displaying the Scotch thistle entwined with a ribbon and specially made for the occasion. Through the *Aberdeen Journal* six hundred pounds had been collected for the men in Bedford. After the Lord Provost's speech, Mr Hector Gordon sang the Hogmanay song and the chorus was taken up very lustily. The soldiers then mounted the chairs and sang *Auld Lang Syne* with great gusto. *God Save the King* followed and the crowd at 9.50 turned out singing and in good humour but quite orderly.

The account in Bewsher's *History of the 51st Highland Division* states that the Division kept Hogmanay, much to the amusement of the people of the town. Dinners were held at most officers' messes, and reels were danced in the market square at midnight in which it was said that the Chief Constable of Bedfordshire himself, Major Stevens, took part. Then *Auld Lang Syne* was sung and the men of various units were played to their billets by their pipers. The whole proceeding was most orderly and witnessed by many of the leading townspeople in evening dress, while the men were under complete control by the Assistant Provost Marshal.

The Diary Continues

Jan. 2nd 1915 We had a short route march today over bad roads.

Sunday Jan. 3rd We had a church parade at 8.15 when a service was held in St Paul's Methodist Church. It was a day of universal prayer on behalf of the Red Cross Society. A form of prayer was read out for the present distress.

Monday Jan. 4th We had an early parade at 8.10 which changed into an emergency move. The rain kept our part of the division from going on the route march. We got wet as it was, standing about waiting for orders. I got inoculated the second time at 6 p.m. It was slightly more painful than the first but my arm got better sooner. I went out at night.

January 5th I was on sick parade owing to inoculation. I had a long lie in the morning up to 7.15 a.m. I felt much the better for it. I went out at night and went for a walk round the town. There was nothing of any interest to be seen.

January 6th Again sick parade. We had a room inspection at 11.30. I have been reading *John Inglesant* [a historical novel by Joseph Henry Shorthouse, published in 1818] and have just finished the first volume. It is extremely interesting and is the first philosophical romance I can ever remember reading. Life here seems to go on with a monotonous routine. There is not much quiet to be got. I find that it is a wonderfully happy life. Things are so easily forgotten. I expect to be in Bedford for a long time yet. We are making ourselves exceedingly comfortable in our present billet. The weather is much milder now, and the sun is shining brightly. I have not washed or shaved today and feel very dirty, so I must set about cleaning now.

Thursday 7th Jan Again on sick parade for inoculation. My arm I thought would be better of an extra day. I had not to see the doctor as sick parade was at 6 p.m. for the next day. The day passed quickly cleaning equipment and helping the cook to peel spuds. The Battalion returned about 4 p.m. having been out in drizzling rain since 7.15 a.m. It was a very bad day they had and I was very glad I had got sick parade.

January 8th Today has been most interesting. I shall set down what happened. Reveille 6.30, breakfast 7.15, parade 10.20. We formed up in Lindon Road at 10.45 and marched off before 11 o'clock. We marched down to the railway and practised entraining and detraining. I had to help to put the cook's wagon in a truck. There were ten of us and we had to rush the lorry up an incline and then get it on to the truck. Everything, tool carts etc. was on the train in ten minutes. I think the C.O. was very pleased. Then we all got into the train, ten to every carriage. The men were in good spirits all the time. It was a beautiful day with strong sunshine and not very cold. The detraining was accomplished in quick time and we were ready to march off by 12.35 p.m. We got back to our company parade ground at 12.55 and had dinner at 1.15. Long dress [long puttees to be worn] went as soon as we had finished dinner and we paraded again at 2 p.m. George Adam Smith, Principal of Aberdeen University, came and looked at us on parade. We passed him as we were marching home in the forenoon. In the afternoon we proceeded to area B and put in an hour of platoon drill. It was new to us all and the NCOs and officers were not very well up in it. We managed to get a fine mess of mud. We got back by 4 o'clock and had pay parade.

Tea was at five, and we had a visit from Principal Smith who made a speech to us. He was very short and seemed rather at a loss for words. The men received him very quietly as Captain Mackinnon was with him. The speech he made was not very pointed. He wished us God-speed and a safe return if we went to the front. He said he expected to see us again as he would be visiting his son in London (his son is home wounded). He told us not to be discouraged that we were kept so long here. There are various ways of serving our country and each part is vitally necessary to the whole organism.

The stress of the situation was somewhat relieved when Lance-Corporal [William] Asher called for three cheers for the Principal and he got right hearty ones. He also tried to relieve the strain himself by saying that he would have to address an overflow meeting upstairs. We have two mess rooms, neither being large enough for the whole company. Before he went he also assured the men that the University would consider each case individually of those who had gone on service, and no man would be hardly dealt with according to the regulations they had been able to make. He interviewed several men privately afterwards, I believe it was because they had applied for commissions.

Principal George Adam Smith

Principal Sir George Adam Smith

Sir George Adam Smith, Principal of the University of Aberdeen, lost two sons in the war. The elder, 2nd Lieutenant George Buchanan Smith, MA, LLB, was severely wounded at Kemmel in December 1914 and spent three months in St Thomas's Hospital in London. He rejoined the 2nd Battalion of the Gordon Highlanders in France and was killed in action near Hulluch on that terrible day for the 2nd Gordons in the battle of Loos on 25th September 1915. His brother Captain Robert Dunlop Smith, who had also been a member of U Company before he joined the regular army in 1912, was later killed in action with the 33rd Punjabis in East Africa on June 12th 1917. The Principal was greatly affected by the loss of George and after walking alone in the Chanonry in Old Aberdeen one October evening soon after the battle he returned home and wrote the following lines.

37

Old Aberdeen, October 1915

Mother of trees and towers and ancient ways
And homes of studious peace; to whose grey Crown
Thy lads come up through these October days,
Come up again the while thy leaves fall down
Rustling about the young and eager feet,
As if the spirits of thy crowded past
Mustering on high those latest ranks to greet
Did down their ghostly salutations cast.

Ah, this October many come no more
Whose trysted faces we had looked to see.
For on the fields of Flanders or that shore
Steep and fire-swept of grim Gallipoli
They fell like leaves, innumerably fell
And though still quick and keen and fain for life,
With as ripe ease and gentleness of will,
As the sere leaf from out the tempest's strife -
Ready for Death and their young sacrifice
By faith in God, by love of home and land,
And the proud conscience of the ungrudged price
Their fathers paid at Freedom's high demand.

Through thy stripped trees trailing with the mist
The mournful music of the pipes comes creeping,
Mourn thou not those who only failed thy Tryst
Because they kept a Holier - and are keeping.

The Diary Continues

Saturday 9th Jan. Today the orders were a divisional route march along parallel roads conveying towards the same place. We marched out about 9.15 from Lansdowne Road and went along St Peters Street, turned to the right and then went out about five miles when we had a long cold wait of several hours. During the wait there was a good deal of horseplay, both among the officers and men. It threatened rain for a little just before, but now it was bright and clear and cold. When we started again we passed a sign post registering five and a half miles to Bedford and again another the same distance. By the time we got back we must have covered about fourteen or fifteen miles. We got back at six o'clock - a very long parade. I felt very hungry and for a little slightly squeamish for want of food. One thing I find is that hunger disappears if it is not satisfied at the time. One gets past being hungry. I had on my army boots for the first time and felt my feet very sore as I was getting near home. When we got back we found that those recruits who had gone to Tamworth for musketry had returned. Today I got four shillings for the wear and tear of my civilian clothes while I was in Aberdeen. I was really entitled to the full seven and sixpence, but the Government never pays more than it can help.

Preparedness for War

Knowles' comment on kit and boots is further evidence of the lack of even the most elementary preparation for war in Britain in 1914. Like so many other soldiers who rejoined the colours after the outbreak of the war, Knowles had to wear his civilian clothes for some time and was not issued with ammunition boots until January of 1915. This was not at all unusual and other Gordons have described gruelling route marches at Bedford and returning to billets with blistered feet and blood-soaked shoes. Some old soldiers from Glasgow who had previously served with the 4th Gordons rejoined attired in civilian suits and bowler hats, and did all their drill in that dress. To keep up their morale, some Gordon battalions were instructed to send home for their crimson tunics and they then proceeded to cut a dash in their smart uniforms with the metal tigers of Mysore on the collar, the yellow facings on the jacket, and the white spats and black buttons - the latter in memory of Sir John Moore of Corunna. Moore, who was born in Glasgow, was sent out to command the British forces in Portugal against Napoleon and was killed in a rearguard action against the French at Corunna and buried on the field of battle.

The 6th Gordons

One month before Knowles' comment about his boots the 6th Gordons had arrived at the front in Belgium near Hazebrouck in the first week of December 1914 - the first battalion of the 51st Highland Division to do so - where they relieved the 1st Battalion of the Grenadier Guards in the line. The Gordons went into waterlogged muddy trenches wearing kilts, hose, spats and shoes and a number of men lost their shoes in the mud and were unable to recover them. Captain David MacKenzie noted that many of his men returned from a tour in the front line bare from the knee downwards, and in three instances even kilts were lost. He recalled that the spirits of the men were not dampened - rather their anger against the enemy was increased by their plight. He illustrated this with the story of the sturdy, stocky piper who withdrew his legs from the mud stripped of hose and shoes and shouted, 'the next German band that I see in Bucksburn, I'll ca' ma fit through the bloody drum'. The reaction of the Grenadiers was summed up by the man who said to his mate, 'Cor blimey, the King's Grenadiers being relieved by a blinking Territorial mob'.

The men who lost their shoes used some sandbags to cover their feet, but after four days of duty in the front line in December they were all suffering from frostbite. When they returned to billets after being relieved they found that some pairs of boots had been sent up for them, but even a size larger than usual was found to be painful. At that time the remedy supplied to the troops for frost-bitten feet was whale oil. Things began to improve a little at this time with the issue of thigh-length gumboots - two to a platoon - and sheepskin jerkins. Perhaps the presence of the Prince of Wales, who was serving behind the lines - much to his disgust - with the 1st Grenadier Guards in the Sailly district and was frequently seen by the Gordons, had some effect on their supplies. The shortage of boots paled into insignificance, however, compared with the shortage of shells for the guns to fire. The Germans had been making munitions for many years and were able to fire shells continuously at the British positions while the British had to content themselves with a ration of so many rounds per day. Many soldiers not unnaturally considered this state of affairs to be nothing short of scandalous.

CHAPTER THREE

Measles, a Dance and a Truce

BACK at Bedford, the Highland Division began to suffer casualties from an unexpected source which Knowles recorded in his diary.

January 10th Sunday Church parade at St Martin's 12.30. In the evening went up with Scott to Charles Buchan who is doing Guild work here. Met the chaplain of the 6th Seaforths whose name is Reid.

Monday 11th Jan. Paraded at 9.10 and marched out Bromham way for five miles to Stevington. Then back a mile and fell out for several hours. It was very cold and I got a slight cold sitting on damp grass. Over fifty per cent of the people of Bedford have colds just now. Measles is also raging in the schools and among the troops. Several men have died of them. It must be very unhealthy here with so many insanitary houses, and so many people in each house. The town is low lying and far from exhilarating. We were the reserve of the Gordon Brigade which was the third line of reserves to the division. The Argyll and Sutherland Highlanders were in the fighting line. All this divisional work provides training for the officers, and the men learn nothing at all.

4th Gordons crossing Bromham Bridge

Measles in the Highland Division

The outbreak of infectious disease in October 1914 among the children of Bedford and its rapid spread to the Highlanders took the local population by surprise. There was considerable anxiety about the number of soldiers infected and the necessity to move whole battalions into quarantine. When military funerals began the town was soon swept by rumours that the troops were being neglected and that hundreds were dying, particularly from measles.

In November 1914 the Medical Officer for Health for Bedford reported that in the previous two months there had been 32 cases of scarlet fever and 25 of diphtheria, of which 16 cases of scarlet fever and 12 of diphtheria had been notified by the military. All the military cases had been admitted to the Isolation Hospital. In view of the conditions in Bedford with the population about fifty per cent above its normal level, and the peculiar susceptibility of some of the Highland troops to measles, the MOH recommended that measles should be made a compulsory notifiable disease during the stay of the military in the town. The failure to produce figures for the outbreak of the disease amongst the troops did not in any way allay the anxiety and the following letter appeared in the *Bedfordshire Times* on 1 January 1915.

Deaths Among the Scottish Soldiers

New Year's Eve 1914

Sir,
It is most depressing to hear on all sides of the number of deaths among our Scottish Territorials. Pneumonia following upon measles! That is what we are told. Is it surprising if measles are neglected in the early stages of the disease that by the time the men are sent into hospital pneumonia has already set in and there is very little chance of their recovery? Is this state of things to be allowed to go on in our midst and no one raise a voice against it?

Your obedient servant
A Bedford Householder

[We have received many enquiries on the subject and there is little question as to the strong feeling about it in Bedford. The difficulty is for private individuals to take any step which will not do as much harm as good. Many are helping as they find opportunity by giving warmth, food and garments to the sick, but it is surely not impossible so to organise the resources, public and private, which are available to give our gallant Scottish guests the care and attention that civilians would receive in similar cases of illness. Ed.]

The army authorities decided to act to quell the disquiet and on 15 January the *Bedfordshire Times* carried a leading article on the subject.

So many rumours have been prevalent of late, many of them grossly exaggerated, as to the number of deaths of Scottish Territorials, that it seems desirable to give the actual figures. These are supplied by Major Keble, the Deputy Director of Medical Services to the Highland Division, and are the vital statistics relating to the Division from August 1914 to mid-January 1915. There have been three deaths from Scarlet Fever, three from Diphtheria and twenty-seven from Measles. These figures should at once put a stop to all the talk of 'hundreds of deaths'. The average number of troops quartered in and around Bedford during the past five months has been about 17,500 and the total number of deaths works out at 2.2 per thousand men. The real difficulty as to measles arises in the case of men like the Camerons who come from the Western Highlands and Isles where such diseases are unknown, and they have no resisting power as is built up in town-bred populations which for generations have been subject to the disease. All that can be done is done. The men who have been in contact with measles and are susceptible are removed to the Huts at Howbury. Then if they are attacked, they are removed to the measles hospitals. The official medical view is that the number of deaths is not large under the circumstances and all the evidence goes to show that they are right.

There followed a list of the 416 cases of measles by battalion which bears out the statement about the Camerons. The 4th Camerons had 141 cases of measles with 14 deaths and the 8th Argylls had 101 cases with 4 deaths. The Camerons suffered more severely than any other unit in the Highland Division and by the end of the epidemic 28 men had died and at least the same number had been discharged as unfit for further military service. Many of the men came from homes in the remotest glens and hamlets in the far north of Scotland where measles was either unknown or had not been seen for generations. Infectious diseases were spread by occasional visitors from the cities, but the difficulty of travel meant that they seldom appeared in remote areas of the Highlands. The 6th Gordons (who came from Banffshire) had three deaths among their 33 measles sufferers, but the 4th, 5th and 7th Gordons had only 12 cases and no deaths. Twenty-five cases of measles a day were being admitted to hospital at the height of the epidemic of 1914-15, but by the end of January it was showing signs of abating. The final total of measles cases in the division was 529 with 65 deaths.

The return of the Argyll and Sutherland Highlanders from quarantine changed the appearance of the Bunyan canteen which was again thronged each night with noisy and cheerful troops, and the amount of porridge consumed was described as remarkable. On Friday and Saturday nights there was usually a programme of music with such favourites as *Jean from Aberdeen, A Blessing, My Ain Folk* and *Where my caravan has rested*, and many favourite hymns were sung heartily, led by members of the Bunyan choir. Drummer Wilson frequently delighted the audience with humorous songs of his own composition, especially the clever verses about *Stew, Stew, Stew.*

Dr David Rorie of Cults

In January the Argylls celebrated with a concert the opening of their new Brigade recreation hall at Goldington Road in Bedford, the work on which had been superintended by the Reverend Herbert Reid with the United Free Church of Scotland Guild in Bedford. The opening night was crowded and Brigadier St John Burton made a witty speech which was replied to in a song of his own composition by Major David Rorie, the general practitioner from Cults in Aberdeenshire who was with the 1st Highland Field Ambulance in Bedford. The song was called 'I'm sure ye ken that a' through the Brigade' and was sung to the tune *The Laird o' Cockpen*. The last verse ran:

> *An' the last thing, I tell ye, the reason I'm here*
> *Is because I've got orders frae oor Brigadier*
> *If he gies ye an order, it maun be obeyed*
> *An' I'm sure ye ken that a' through the Brigade*

Dr David Rorie's poetic talents had made him a well-known figure in the Aberdeen area and much further afield. Born in Edinburgh in 1867, he received his early education at Aberdeen Collegiate School and then spent a year in the arts faculty at the University of Aberdeen before graduating in medicine at Edinburgh. He held a variety of medical posts before settling down as a general medical practitioner in Cults in 1905 at the age of 38. Rorie was a very sociable man and a considerable poet whose efforts were recognised in a signal fashion in 1930 by the Aberdeen Medico-Chirurgical Society when they appointed him their Poet Laureate. He is probably best remembered for his poem set to music *The Lum Hat Wantin' The Croon* which was sung in the Boer War and by Scottish troops in Flanders, and for many years now has been sung at their annual dinner by the members of the Medico-Chirurgical Society.

Rorie had a very distinguished army career, largely due to his great organising ability, and was noted for his bravery. He was appointed Assistant Director of Medical Services to the 51st Highland Division in 1917, was twice mentioned in despatches and awarded the DSO as well as the French Legion of Honour. He was the organiser and writer of many sketches for the 51st Highland Division concert party known as *The Balmorals* which entertained many Scottish battalions when they were resting out of the line.

The Balmorals

News from the Front

The censors saw to it that there was a paucity of war news from France for the newspapers. What little news there was appeared in extracts from 'Letters from the Front' which were published each week in the *Bedfordshire Times*, and some of the letters cannot have helped to lift the spirits of U Company. There was also an early indication of the limitations of medical and surgical treatment of the wounded in the Great War with the publication in November 1914 of a gloomy piece about Captain Frank Pope of Sandy, near Bedford. He had been wounded in the leg, and although the surgeons tried to save the limb they could not do so, and he now had no left arm and no right leg below the knee. This was certainly a taste of things to come. As a result of the severe censorship there was an absence of fresh and immediate news of the fighting at the front, and it is not surprising that the national and local newspapers had been giving prominence to tales of German atrocities. Many of these stories had proved very difficult to authenticate, but were published nonetheless and the *Bedfordshire Times* carried a third leader on 11 September 1914.

A Bedford Lady and German Cruelties

A Bedford lady who is down in France on her honeymoon has written home as follows. We are thinking of coming home as soon as travelling is easier, but at present only sixty pounds of luggage is allowed and it would mean leaving everything behind. After a description of fifty Belgian refugees who had arrived in the village, she went on to say that she had been talking to one of the women refugees and had asked her if the newspaper accounts of German brutality were true. She replied that they were more like savages that human beings, and that they had killed little children by snatching them from their mother's arms, piercing them with their bayonets and then hacking them to bits.

On the same date as the above appeared an account was given also of the wounded from France arriving at Wrest Park. Wrest House was the home of Lord Lucas, and part of it had been converted into a convalescent home. The wounded men told of how the Germans at Mons had turned and fled at the sight of the British bayonet, in spite of having an advantage of about ten to one. They were emphatic in condemning the cruelty of the Germans who were not content with torturing the wounded by depriving them of eyesight or otherwise maiming them, but who did not hesitate to kill their own wounded or even burn their corpses in the corn fields. The men of the Highland Division can scarcely have been encouraged by reading such accounts of the war.

For some time Belgian refugees in London had been finding accommodation in and around Bedford, and in November the newspaper reported that there were rumours that somewhere in the neighbourhood there was a Belgian child with both its hands cut off. This handless child was supposed to be in the vicinity of Wooton but the people of the village denied any knowledge of such a child. A similar story was told in Morayshire in Scotland where, on the previous week, the Reverend Dr Macpherson addressed a recruiting march at the plainstones in Elgin and told his listeners of a family in Huntly who had offered to take two Belgian girls in to their service, only to discover that the hands of those poor girls had been cut off. The editor of the *Bedfordshire Times* decided that there had been enough gloom and was happy to carry a report from *The Times* of London of a letter from an officer in a Highland regiment who gave a most graphic picture of life in the trenches, and described dugouts which were roofed, walled and floored to make them habitable. He thought the food was wonderfully good, the bill of fare including chicken, *paté de foie gras*, plum puddings and cake. But the conditions were said to be dirty and when clothes were changed they had to be boiled.

The Diary Continues

Tuesday 12th Jan. We got the morning off in order to clean equipment and billets. First there was a kit inspection. Then the afternoon parade was cancelled after short dress [short puttees to be worn] had blown. A football match was hurriedly arranged between U and G companies. I acted as linesman. Score 2-1 for G.

Wednesday 13th Jan. Another divisional day. Parade 9.10 a.m. We marched out six miles and then got the order to return to billets, leaving one battalion to take up a position. We got back by 2.15 instead of 4 o'clock as was expected. There is a feeling of spring in the air today. This is the first time for long that I have felt really warm on the march. The sun was quite bright and seemed to give out heat. Some of the good people of Bedford find great difficulty in understanding the Scottish dialect. A very broad spoken Scotsman went up to a refreshment stall and asked in a loud voice for tuppence worth of snaps. The woman asked him what he wanted and he said snaps. Then she handed him a packet of Woodbine cigarettes which are in great request here

A Highland Battalion in Bedford marches past John Bunyan's statue

as everywhere. When he refused these and got her to understand what he wanted, she apologised and said she didn't know what he said, and just risked the Woodbines (which have various appellations). Rather a good joke since it is perfectly true.

Thursday 14th Jan. Today we had an emergency practice move and in the afternoon went down to the Midland Station and practised entraining and detraining. At six o'clock I went on sick parade as I had a cold. The doctor sounded me and pronounced it influenza.

Saturday 16th Jan. I got up this morning slightly better, so went on parade. The orders were emergency practice. We got a hundred rounds of ammunition, field dressing, iron ration, pay book and identity disc served out. We also had to roll up blankets ready for moving and get a full pack together. Then we paraded at 10 a.m. and went out by Bromham and right round Bedford to Elstow where we passed the little house where John Bunyan was born. It is quite a tiny cottage with four small front windows, two upstairs and two down. Just along a little on the opposite side is the Bunyan Memorial Church. We got back about 2 p.m. and had tea about four and late dinner at five-thirty which I did not attend for a wonder. A great number of U Company are applying for commissions. Perhaps I shall myself, though I like being a private well enough and it gives a better experience of men, though there is not very much about military matters to be learned. [This was an echo of the earlier crisis and showed that the vexed question of commissions had not gone away].

Sunday 17th Jan. Church parade 9.30, billets scrubbed 12.30. Afternoon wrote letters. Bromham Road Wesleyan at 6.30 – Dr Barber of Cambridge; thirty years ago went out to Korea.

18th January The rumour that we are leaving for the front soon seems sure enough. Today we had only to see about getting our equipment complete. I am down with a nasty dose of the flu and asked for the doctor to come and see me. It is now 8 p.m. and I might have been dead for all the attention I have received. A billet is no place to be seriously ill. I saw a man Scott of the 6th Gordons tonight and he told me he was off

Bunyan's Cottage

Elstow High Street

ten days with pneumonia. It was four days before the doctor discovered what was wrong with him. The 4th Gordons, 4th Camerons and 8th Argyll and Sutherlands are under orders. [To go to France.]

Tuesday 19th January Saw the doctor at 5 p.m. and got my chest examined. I was pronounced perfectly sound.

46

Wednesday 20th January We went a fifteen mile route march from 9.15 a.m. till 2 o'clock. Our rifles are being numbered so we had a hundred rounds of ball ammunition instead. It was raining all the time nearly, not heavy at first but finally blowing quite a blizzard. As we were coming into Bedford the sky got black and threatening. We all understood what was the cause.

21st January Got up this morning by 6.30 and found about an inch of snow on the ground. It was bitterly cold though not a hard frost. We had rifle inspection at 9 a.m. and then no parade was declared. We have to practise 'internal economy'. I expect to get home on Monday night. I am not letting anyone know yet in case a disappointment should come. There is little doubt now that we are going to France. Everything seems to point that way. I was medically examined and passed as fit for foreign service today at 2.30. In the orders at 9.20 p.m. a list of thirty-nine names were read out as having been selected for furlough. The train was to leave Bedford for Aberdeen on Sunday at 9.15 p.m. and we were to parade at 8.15 with kit bags. I went to bed and could hardly get sleep for thinking how good it was to get home and all the things I am going to do.

Saturday 22nd Jan. Today we had a march to a place on the way to Stevington about three miles outside Bedford and had platoon drill. It was a beautiful park with fine trees in it. The ground was very wet and we got our feet all splashed. About 11.15 we continued our march and went further out, returning through Clapham. This made our march about ten miles besides the drill. Got back about 1.30 and had dinner. I set about getting my kit ready for going home when I heard that fourteen of us were scored out of the list. This included all recruits and those who have but lately arrived. I feel very disappointed but perhaps it is all for the best. I feel it all the more as many from other companies who came down with me have already been home. The reason given is that it would mean too many away at once – a very poor reason. I am glad I have not written home telling them to expect me. There is some word of a third batch going on Friday night and I shall certainly go with it; but its chances of going are at present somewhat vague. I would rather I had never been told I was getting home.

Sunday 23rd January No church parade today. Usual billets inspection. At night I went and heard the Rev Mr Haughton at St Paul's Wesleyan – he was very good.

Monday 24th January 7.30 Running and rapid marching. Breakfast at 8 a.m. Parade 9.15. Double company drill at Stagsden four miles out. We pulled up branches and made a primitive bridge over a stream. No afternoon parade.

Tuesday 25th January Parade 9 a.m. Double company and extended order drill at area A. Then we marched out an extra mile and came back when a surprise awaited us. The adjutant looked very excited. Fourteen men were asked to leave in three-quarters of an hour. Where they went to I do not know even yet – rumour has it they have gone to St Ives. The rest of us were told to get ready to move at a moment's notice but nothing has come of it.

[Rumour was frequently a lying jade in the war but in this case it was true. The fourteen men, with Sergeant J K Forbes in charge *had* gone to search for spies. They were sent to the neighbourhood of St Ives to keep watch on and patrol some roads which were said to be used by German spies going about their business. However, they were unable to confirm the presence of spies in the area and they returned to Bedford to re-join U Company in time for the move to France].

U Company held a dance in Crofton Rooms, St Cuthbert Street. Some ladies had done all the arranging and most men went single. Some of the best people in Bedford were there and several officers. Most of the ladies went home alone in taxis – it was quite enjoyable and I only missed three dances. The men dressed in kilts and sporrans, hose tops, black socks and slippers – no equipment or spats. The chief objection to the affair was that the ladies were too swagger for common soldiers, though not a bit stiff. One of my partners told me she had examined some of our trenches at Stagsden while out hunting. [The local hunt was the Oakley Hunt].

Wednesday 26th January I was very sleepy after the dance but got up at 7.30 in time for the running and rapid marching. It took a good deal out of me as I had been dancing almost continuously from 6-11 the night before. Parade at 9 a.m. and a hard forenoon up to 12.30 at double company, extended order and arm, and battalion drill. There were only thirty-three of U Company on parade so we were a platoon short. No word of the fourteen who left yesterday while twelve are on machine gun section and over twenty on leave. We paraded again at 2 p.m. and marched round by Biddenham and got back for tea at 7.30. This has been a heavy day, especially after a dance. No word of getting home leave yet and there is a rumour that we are to go into an isolation camp on Thursday 4th February. This makes the prospect of leave more precarious still.

U Company's Dance

The dance on 25 January referred to by Knowles in his diary was fully reported in the Women's Number of *Alma Mater* on 3 February 1915.

According to Colour-Sergeant Pratt in his remarks at the end, the much-thought-of function was an 'unqualified success'. We are, without apologising, about to qualify the success with adjective and comment, all laudatory and uncritical. Fortunately, you in Aberdeen are in the same box as ourselves. The dearth of dances is as keen there as here, and you are privileged to sympathise with our glee at the prospect, and our wholehearted *abandon* in throwing ourselves into the festive spirit. [Dances, suppers and dinners were forbidden at Aberdeen University at this stage of the Great War.] On Tuesday we were much perturbed in soul by an alarm which threatened the very life of the 'hop', and actually deprived us of merry knaves, valuable helps, and funny fellows, Low, Lamb, Still, 'Sunny', we reluctantly counted among the absent, but the Dance went on.

[This was a reference to the fourteen men under Sergeant J K Forbes who had been sent to St Ives to search for German spies. 'Sunny' was Private Duncan McLellan, the arts student from Brechin, whose keen sense of humour and fund of good stories earned him the nickname among his peers of 'Sunny Jim'. Private Sydney Still, who had been an enthusiastic member of U Company for five years, did not go to France with the Company. He was discharged as medically unfit in March 1915 and graduated MA in the same year.]

Everything was ripping, the music was good, maybe not so good as Kennaway's, but the floor knocked the much danced-on students' rendezvous into a cocked hat. We all went with a few misgivings, most of us didn't know a soul, but thanks to the Committee, especially the ladies, programmes were soon filled, and after the first half-hour zest and ease were the order of the evening.

The girls – but there, why sandpaper the sensitive souls of our last year's partners!! Enough to hint that they lived up to English-beauty reputation, and that they make few mistakes in dress; that the sitting-out accommodation was ample and evidently attractive. Any other particulars (we have, you notice, given none!) will be given by the indolently or amorously inclined. Colonel Ogilvie was unable to be with us, but sent us a nice note wishing us a good evening. Both our Lieutenants were off on leave, but our Captain and Mrs Mackinnon were there helping the chaperones and adding grace to the picturesqueness of the uniforms and dresses.

Asher, Hawes and McLean made more or less efficient MCs. The really useful workers were the promoters of the dance, ladies all! To them belongs all the credit, and the Company feels very grateful to them for an evening of rare enjoyment, and for a rich store of pleasant memories to carry Flanders-ward. Mollison and Chalmers played an extra reel in the true spirit. The violinist, a wee chap with a big look and a grand air, was almost as funny as the violinist at the last U Company dance in Aberdeen. We almost asked Hawes to play us a waltz, but spared the professional artiste's feelings. The pianist was excellent, only of course, she wasn't Miss Stewart.

Two flappers strayed in and were welcomed eagerly by Warren. Philip's partners (3) turned up, but the inviter's courage failed apparently. C Reid danced a little and sat out a lot, with evident relish. Cooper, Asher and Crichton toed the line from time to time: mostly they were just busy being searched for. In the latter respect, Middleton and 'Jus' [Private John Shanks who wrote prose and verse for *Alma Mater* as 'Jus'] deserve honourable mention. Colour-Sergeant Pratt radiated smiles from corner to corner, and made a nice speechlet (already quoted from) at the end. The buffet was a dream, only there was no time to do it justice. Some of the ladies wanted us to be hungry, and reminded us of the few delicacies we were accustomed to. The programme consisted of twelve waltzes, some one-steps and two-steps, two eightsomes and four lancers. The violinist was very pleased with his '*Devil* among the Tailors', and it was the first eightsome which warmed away the last vestige of freezing.

It was all very charming. We were much too proper to have real 'Twilights' but we had one light put out for realism and for old time's sake. It is hopeless to try and tell you how delightful it was; I don't think we even regretted it wasn't Kennaway's. Next day we were all on parade as fresh as paint, and now we are in that sweet mood when we wish to have our cake and eat it too.

The Diary Continues

Thursday 27th January Orders as yesterday except no night-trenching. In the forenoon parade I had practice in bayonet fighting; the get-up reminded me of a Roman gladiator. [The masks and cuirasses worn at Bedford were not used in France]. Then we had drill and running and the afternoon was filled up with battalion drill in area B. Our applications for leave are in today; probably we shall leave on Saturday night, though something may intervene.

Friday 28th January Was on supply depot work from 8 a.m. to 1 p.m. We had to follow the cooks wagon and load and unload, bringing supplies for the battalion and distributing them to company headquarters. At 6 p.m. paraded as quarter guard at Lansdowne Road. My turn was from eight to ten at night and the same in the morning, there being six of us and a sergeant. We had to sleep on the floor with one blanket and there was a very poor fire so it was rather cold. Very little sleep did I get.

Saturday 29th January Was dismissed from guard at 6 p.m. having been on for twenty-four hours.

Sunday 30th January Church parade at 8.30. Went to communion service in Bunyan Hall at 3 p.m. - a memorable service, being the first held here for the Highland Division in Bedford. Paraded at 8.15 to go on furlough. Train left Bedford at 9.15 p.m. and we got to Aberdeen at 10.45 a.m. It was a very uneventful journey.

Saturday 6th Feb. Returned from furlough. We left Aberdeen at 6.50 last night and on the journey we saw the searchlights at the Forth Bridge. It was an impressive and beautiful spectacle, showing how careful a vigilance has to be kept.

The Christmas Truce of 1914

On the February day that Knowles returned to Bedford from his leave in Aberdeen the *Bedfordshire Times* carried an extract from a letter from the front which

U Company must have read with some incredulity. They were later to be given a first-hand account by one of the 6th Gordons who had been present at the truce. The letter read in part:-

> We have gone back to the trenches now and it is a sight. The North Staffords named it Dead Man's Alley, graves everywhere. If you dig a spit or two you dig some poor chap up - I did the other day. But there are a decent lot of fellows in front of us now - Saxons; they don't like the Prussian Guards. They haven't fired a shot since the day before Christmas nor have we. I believe they will surrender. Our trenches are only eighty yards apart and we meet each other halfway and give them tins of jam for cigars. It seems strange but it is true. [This last statement is corroborated by information we have received from another source. Ed.]

After bloody battles which had cost the British and French some 50,000 casualties, a strange and quite extraordinary event, without parallel in military history, took place at Christmas 1914. At the time it happened attempts were made to keep it out of the newspapers, and so from the general public by the vigilance of the censor, but letters sent home from the front at the time do not appear to have been censored. The London *Sphere*, which had a small circulation, published an account of the truce and the *Daily Mirror* also managed to defeat the censor with a picture on its front page of British and German troops posing together for a photograph. This now well-authenticated Christmas truce occurred along lengthy areas of the British line and was said, in some parts, to have carried on for a week or more. It certainly took place on a part of the front held by the 2nd Battalion of the Gordons, and also by the 6th Gordons whose padre was the Reverend J Esslemont Adams, minister of the West United Free Church in Aberdeen. He was one of the first to contact the Germans and make sure that the truce could be made use of to bury the dead.

A very graphic description of what took place was contained in a letter home from Captain A D (Micky) Chater of the 2nd Gordons who were then attached to the 7th Division. Chater was born in 1890 and educated at Harrow School. In 1909 he volunteered for service in the Artists Rifles and as a corporal in that regiment he advanced towards the front as far as Bailleul in 1914 in some of the old red London buses - the entire British army at that time had fewer than 80 motor vehicles. Many of these buses were driven by their own civilian drivers and that is why, today, representatives of London Transport march in their uniforms in the annual Armistice Day parade. After the casualties sustained in the first battle of Ypres in October and November of 1914 there was an urgent call for officers, and in his papers lodged in the Imperial War Museum in London Chater describes how he 'volunteered rashly' and was posted to the 2nd battalion of the Gordons. He was severely wounded in the lower jaw on 11 March 1915 at Neuve Chapelle and convalesced in Lady Hadfield's hospital established in the Grand Hotel at Wimereux, on the French coast just north of Boulogne. His case was reported in *The Lancet* and attracted a great deal of attention as his jaw had been set by the unqualified French-American Charles Valadier who was widely regarded by members of the medical profession as a quack, and they were astounded by his success.

Chater's papers recalled how the Christmas truce started as a burial party and service for those who had recently been killed, but that the High Command soon told them to get on with the war. Opposite the 2nd Gordons were the Saxons who, he says, hated fighting and gave them warning when the Prussian Guards were coming into the line. The immediacy of his letter to his mother makes it all the more striking.

Christmas Day

Dearest Mother,

I am writing this in the trenches in my dug-out – with a wood fire going and plenty of straw it is rather cosy, although it is freezing hard and real Christmas weather.

I think I have seen one of the most extraordinary sights today that anyone has ever seen. About ten o'clock this morning I was peeping over the parapet when I saw a German waving his arms and presently two of them got out of their trenches and came towards ours. We were just going to fire on them when we saw they had no rifles, so one of our men went out to meet them and in about two minutes the ground between the two lines of trenches was swarming with men and officers of both sides shaking hands and wishing each other a Happy Christmas. This continued for about half an hour when we were ordered back to the trenches.

It is really very extraordinary that this sort of thing should happen in a war in which there is so much bitterness and ill-feeling. The Germans in this part of the line are certainly sportsmen if they are nothing else. Of course I don't suppose it has happened everywhere along the line, although I think that indiscriminate firing was more or less stopped in most places on Christmas day. We are down in billets now until the 30th December when we go up again, and so it [the war] appears to be going on. We have had very few casualties lately and only two killed in the last three weeks or so, though we have had a certain number wounded; and we had another party with the Germans in the middle. We exchanged cigarettes and autographs and some more people took photos. I don't know how long it will go on for – I believe it was supposed to stop yesterday, but we can hear no firing going on along the front today except a little distant shelling. We are at any rate having another truce on New Year's Day as the Germans want to see how the photos come out.

Yesterday was lovely in the morning and I went for several quite long walks about the lines. It is difficult to realise what that means, but of course in the ordinary way there is not a sign of life above ground and everyone who puts his head up is shot at.

Captain David MacKenzie

Captain David MacKenzie MC, MA, of the 6th Gordons, was the schoolmaster at Cullen in Banffshire both before and after the war and he wrote a vivid account of his battalion's activities in France. In *The Sixth Gordons in France and Flanders*, published in Aberdeen in 1922, he described how it was not unusual for troops in the front-line trenches to hold impromptu concerts when they sang sentimental and patriotic songs and that the Germans did the same. The other side often received these offerings with applause and sometimes called for an encore. The Germans spent Christmas Eve singing carols and shouted to the Jocks that they did not intend to shoot on Christmas day and encouraged them to refrain from violence. Little attention was paid to this but on Christmas morning the British sentries saw a number of Germans standing unarmed in front of their trenches. The padre, the Reverend J Esslemont Adams, and the commanding officer of the 6th Gordons, Lt-Colonel Colin McLean from Alford, had just completed a burial service behind the lines and had come up for the daily inspection.

When the CO saw what was happening he ordered the Gordons to return to their trenches but the chaplain quickly announced that he was off to speak to the Germans to arrange for the burial of the dead on both sides who were lying in No Man's Land. Adams urged the British and German COs to agree to a short religious service after the dead had been buried, and this memorable scene was enacted at four o'clock on Christmas day. Drawn up on one side of No Man's Land were British officers with soldiers in ranks behind them; on the other side were German officers with men of their regiments around them, and in between stood the chaplain, an interpreter, and a German divinity student serving with the Saxons. The chaplain read the twenty-third psalm in English with the German student repeating it after him in German. A short prayer was then read and the chaplain stepped forward and saluted the German commander who shook hands with him and thanked him.

This remarkable episode did not signify the end of the goodwill, and a friendly understanding was reached whereby the troops alerted one another to the approach of senior officers when the war was resumed by firing a few rounds high into the air in case any harm be occasioned to the other side. A number of Germans on the section of the line held by the 6th Gordons were fluent in English – one had been a waiter at the Hotel Cecil – and communication presented little difficulty. Bully beef and jam were exchanged for sausages and chocolate, cigarettes and tobacco for German cigars, and British rum for wine and cognac.

The troops drank one another's health and, in the strangest ritual of all, the barbers serving with the German regiments shaved a number of the Gordons in the middle of No Man's Land. Caution made the opposing sides keep a certain distance from each other's trenches, although there is a story of a wag in the 6th Gordons, who, seeing a bell on the German wire, went over and rang it and requested lunch. On this part of the front the truce lasted for ten days, from Christmas day until 3 January 1915. On the afternoon of that day the end of the truce was formally arranged by both sides and on the following day volleys of rifle fire were ordered. The 2nd Gordons, the 6th Gordons and the 1st Battalion of the Grenadier Guards all fired a *feu de joie* with rifle muzzles high in the air. Immediately afterwards a strange message went along the British front line – 'pass it along, the Kaiser's dead' – and the truce was over.

Still in Bedford

The 4th Gordons continued their training in Bedford and John Knowles described in his diary the examination of their shooting abilities for which U Company had been renowned.

Sunday 7th Feb. Church parade 11.45 when Principal George Adam Smith preached his farewell sermon to the battalion. He dealt with the causes of the war and bid us ever remember in the heart of battle the righteousness of the cause for which we fight. It was not quite what we expected and I was rather disappointed. Billet inspection 10.30 as usual.

Monday 8th Feb. We are now going to fire the soldier's test in musketry. Today we went to Herring's Green range (Cotton End) and fired practice grouping at a hundred yards, and five snap and eight rapid at two hundred yards as in the Territorial test. The conditions were bad, first sunshine right in our eyes and later, wind and rain. We got quite wet and boots muddy as usual.

Tuesday 9th Feb. Reveille 6.30, breakfast 7 and parade 7.30. We had to stand by for the rain. At 2.30 parade for drill, platoon extended orders and musketry. We were issued with two pairs of puttees long and short, khaki hose tops, lanyards, mess tin covers, cartridges, pouches and body belt.

Wednesday 10th Feb. As yesterday parade 7.30. We went to Herring's Green range and fired at five hundred yards as in the Territorial test. I had to find Captain Mackinnon's horse and groom, so followed the others to the range by myself. It was a day of

The Bell (a student haunt) on the way to Cotton End

brilliant sunshine, one of the few I have seen here, and I enjoyed the five mile walk to the full. When we got back orders had been given to pack up ready for moving, but there is nothing definite as yet. We got issued with a second pair of boots at six o'clock.

Thursday 11th Feb. Musketry.

Friday 12th Feb. Musketry.

Saturday 13th Feb. Musketry.

Sunday 14th Feb. Church parade at St Paul's Methodist. Went to Bromham Road in the evening and after the service had an interesting talk with the minister the Rev W H Haughton.

Monday 15th Feb. Musketry in beautiful sunshine. In the evening we had night trenching at Biddenham and got back to tea at 7.30. A long wearisome twelve hour day.

Tuesday 16th Feb. We finished classification test in musketry. The weather was good but hazy and the target very indistinct.

Wednesday 17th Feb. A day of rain and we had to clean up our billets. We are busy getting ready to move. An order came from the Divisional office for us to move on Friday but the adjutant wired back that we could not be ready till Monday. I was very amused to read in the Aberdeen Express of Saturday 13th February that the 4th Gordons were now in an isolation camp. It shows that nothing in the army is certain for the move was put off at the last minute. That we shall say good-bye to Bedford within a week seems almost certain. Visited Elstow at night.

Thursday 18th Feb. Inspection by General Allason of the Division on area B in the afternoon. One of the staff wished us good-bye – we are leaving tomorrow.

Butts field at Herring's Green where U Company practised musketry

Kitchener's Message to his Troops

Every man proceeding on a draft to the front was given a copy of a personal message to his troops written by the Secretary of State for War, Field Marshal Lord (Horatio Herbert) Kitchener. This was to be Lord Kitchener's first and only message to his soldiers.

You are ordered abroad as a soldier of the King to help our French comrades against the invasion of a common enemy. You have to perform a task which will need your courage, your energy, your patience. Remember that the honour of the British Army depends upon your individual conduct. It will be your duty not only to set an example of discipline and perfect steadiness under fire, but also to maintain the most friendly relations with those you are helping in this struggle. The operations in which you are engaged will, for the most part, take place in a friendly country, and you can do your own country no better service than in showing yourself, in France and Belgium, in the true character of a British soldier.

Be invariably courteous, considerate and kind. Never do anything likely to injure or destroy property, and always look upon looting as a disgraceful act. You are sure to meet with a welcome and be trusted; and your conduct must justify that welcome and that trust. Your duty cannot be done unless your health is sound. So keep constantly on your guard against any excesses. In this new experience you may find temptations both in wine and women. You must entirely resist both temptations, and while treating all women with perfect courtesy, you should avoid any intimacy.

Do your duty bravely. Fear God. Honour the King.

Kitchener
Field Marshal

The Diary Continues

Friday 19th Feb. We parade in twenty minutes to go to the station - bound for Southampton. Great excitement. We left Bedford at 9.15 and arrived at Southampton at 2 p.m. There was a coffee stall at the wharf where we stopped, so we got food if we cared to buy it. We then had to hurry out of the shed and do fatigue work on the quay, and in the transport now and then, till six o'clock when we embarked, each company to its proper quarters. Our company had the second lowest deck of the fore-hold and above us were the horses and the hay. It was a fairly roomy place but when we lay down there was not much spare floor space. The main entrance for air was by the hatchway leading into the main deck where the horses were stalled. Beyond this there was only two funnel-shaped ventilators. The worst thing of all was during the night passage when all lights were out – then Dante might have got some ideas for his Inferno. We were fortunate indeed in having an exceptionally smooth passage and only one or two were sick.

We were fed during the passage on bully beef, cheese and hard biscuits. We had tea about seven o'clock, about half an hour after we started, and again in the morning about eight o'clock. We landed off Le Havre about 4 a.m. and there weighed anchor after being examined by searchlights. During our passage we were guarded all the way by a torpedo boat destroyer which could go all round us, while cruisers showed up every now and then. The transport we went across in had originally been a cattle boat, the *Archimedes* of Liverpool, of about eight thousand tons, larger than any boats that come into Aberdeen. We sailed into Le Havre about eleven. It has a magnificent harbour and seems a town of considerable beauty architecturally. We had dinner of concocted soup in the warehouse beside our landing stage. It was much like any other seaport. One part of the shed is occupied by a YMCA where you bought penny tickets to any extent and got equivalent value in food such as tea and coffee, buns, chocolate and cigarettes.

There in charge was the bright and sunny Reverend L McLean Watt of Edinburgh, late of Turriff as he was careful to inform us, who asked if there were any farm loons among us. There are several. Then we marched out to the heights above the town where the camps are situated as resting places. [This was at Bléville, about five miles away]. We had a very hot sun and it was terrible toiling up the hill with all our kit. When we got to the camp we had a long stand about till we got allotted to our several tents. It is a splendid camping ground, high up and breezy though rather inclined to get muddy.

Sergeant-Major Bewick

As U Company, with the rest of the 4th Battalion of the Gordon Highlanders on their way to France, marched through the streets of Bedford to the skirl of the pipes and with their kilts swaying in rhythm, most of them were quite unaware as they passed the County Hospital that it contained the dead body of their Regimental Sergeant-Major. A few days before he had been going about his usual duties of drilling the battalion with all the guile and persuasion and occasional sarcasm of an old regular soldier who had served with the Scots Guards in the South African War. For the past eight years as the Regimental Sergeant-Major of this Battalion of part-time soldiers he had been the military sage of the 4th Gordons, consulted by all ranks from the commanding officer to the most junior NCO as to military procedure, discipline, good order and parade ground drill. The members of U Company had been quick to admit that their new-found proficiency in company and battalion drill was due to their Sergeant-Major who was described as having an excellent drill voice and seeming to know every single man in the battalion. A popular story was that the battalion was so efficiently drilled that on one occasion it came smartly to attention when a dog barked.

Bewick's final illness was short and dramatic, and as so often happened in those days apparently quite unexplained. He was an ostensibly fit and healthy 38 year old soldier who was suddenly taken ill on Monday night, admitted unconscious to hospital on Tuesday morning and died on Wednesday. Thus it came about that the body of the man who more than any other had been largely responsible for bringing the rawest of troops to a high state of readiness and efficiency was being readied for its last resting place while his battalion went off to war.

The *Archimedes* was guarded on its way to France because the Germans had declared, in February of 1915, that the waters around Britain constituted a war zone and that shipping would be sunk on sight by their submarines. They also made it known that the safety of ships from neutral countries could not be guaranteed. This policy led to the sinking of the *Lusitania* off the coast of Ireland in May 1915 with the loss of over a hundred American lives, and consequent vigorous protests from the United States.

CHAPTER FOUR

The Great Adventure

The Diary Continues

Sunday 21st Feb. Reveille 7, breakfast 8, dinner 1 p.m. Usual camp routine, but no parades. We were not allowed to go outside the camp. There were coffee stalls and *vin* shops within the area. Lots of French people came about us and I got a chance of trying my French with but indifferent success though I was understood well enough. At night we got served with fur jackets. [These were to prove a haven for lice].

Monday 22nd Feb. Reveille at 2.15 a.m. breakfast 2.30 and parade 2.45 a.m. – terrific rush. We marched down through the town with no noise under cover of night to the railway station. There seems to be a large number of French troops all over. They have dark blue tunics, lighter trousers with short black leggings and cheese cutter caps. Their guns are very long with long bayonets. The usual height of a French soldier is five feet three inches and the arms look ridiculously disproportionate. We fell out in the station and I fell asleep on the platform and then we had to get into carriages marked *Hommes* 40, *Chevaux* 8. There were thirty-two of us in one carriage and there was little else but cramped limbs, as there was no room to lie out in. The train went fearfully slowly and started with a tremendous jerk and stopped ditto. It has been a beautiful day though frosty and we have no idea where we are going. There has been a collision on the main line so we have gone round by the seaport of Fécamp where we stopped an hour or two. It is a beautiful country and is well called La Belle France. A rumour is out that the British troops have captured Ostend. We are settled down more comfortably in our cattle truck – at least there is plenty of fresh air and straw on the floor makes rather a comfortable bed. *Volets a fermeture interieurs pour changements en douane* is written up inside the truck. The train is going about fifteen miles an hour – worse than the Buchan train.

Captain N C S Down

In a book entitled *Temporary Heroes*, published in London in 1917, N C S Down gives an account of his experiences with the 4th Gordons in France. A copy of this book is held in the Imperial War Museum in London and can be examined only on microfilm. As it was printed during the war it was subject to censorship, and the copy held by the Museum was the one sent to the censor's office prior to publication. His blue pencil has been used heavily throughout the work, indicating what had to be omitted in the final published version; but the censored text can still be read in the museum copy. Much of the censoring has obviously been provoked by the author's sardonic comments on the war and its conduct, as the events of 1915 had long since ceased to be secret. *Temporary Heroes* describes the activities of the 4th Battalion of the Gordons in France and Flanders from February 1915 to July 1916. When the Battalion went to France in February 1915, with very few exceptions, the officers and men of the battalion were Aberdonians or came from the neighbourhood.

The author of *Temporary Heroes*, Captain Norman Cecil Sommers Down, writing under the pseudonym of Cecil Sommers, was one of the exceptions and owed his gazetting as an officer in the Gordons to the help of General Sir Ian Hamilton, himself a Gordon and in 1914 Inspector-General of the Territorial Army. Sir Ian's father and Down's grandfather, Colonel R M Sutherland, had served together for many years in the 92nd Foot, the precursor of the Gordon Highlanders.

Down's writing is wonderfully evocative and his dryly sarcastic sense of humour lightens an account of a terrible experience in grim conditions – and even he cannot hide the grimness. The irreverent wit he brings to bear on the 'brass hats' was severely censored, and his book is a delight to read with its light and witty touch. It is a collection of letters written to 'The Only Phyllis', which serves as the dedication, and his facility with a pen is evident throughout the text. He also sailed from Southampton on the *Archimedes* with the 4th Gordons and his comments on arrival in France are very similar to those of Knowles, although delivered in a lighter vein. With regard to the issue of fur jackets on 21 February, Down describes his own as:

A rather quiet black fox with musquash sleeves or thereabouts, but some of them are in the very latest mode. Lance-Corporal McGregor for instance looks very smart in his leopard skin with collar of skunk and cuffs of polar bear. He is a fish porter to trade. The Commanding Officer's is rather a nice little thing in Persian lamb; touches of domestic cat about the yoke giving it a very chic appearance.

Our debut on foreign soil was marked by a pleasing incident. Our Commanding Officer had never been in France before and neither had the adjutant. So when they saw a figure approaching them arrayed in gorgeous uniform they jumped to the conclusion that it was some French general come to greet us. Accordingly we marched past him at attention with eyes left and the band playing [the regimental march] *Hielan Laddie*. We found out later that he was a private in the local gendarmerie. Still, I expect he enjoyed the experience.

As in much of the book, the postscripts to this letter have been heavily erased with the censor's blue pencil.

PS The boat we came over in was a cold storage boat converted at great expense into a transport. The boat alongside was a transport converted at great expense into a cold storage boat.

PPS We are a great nation.

His description of the subsequent train journey tallies with that of Knowles who likened it to the slow Buchan train. The speed it travelled at enabled some of U Company to get out and trot alongside it to stretch their legs.

Once it really got a move on though we kept up a pretty steady six miles an hour. Of course every time we came to a wayside estaminet the engine driver descended for a glass of vin blanc and a chat, but we all realised that this was war at last and no one complained. As you have probably gathered, we were not on the main line. There had been a big smash somewhere so we were sent on a circular tour round a very hilly and altogether rural loop line. At each little station the villagers crowded round the trucks admiring our kilts and bare blue knees – the kilts I mean.

The journey from Le Havre was made by Fécamp, Dieppe, Boulogne and Calais to Bailleul, south of Ypres, which was at that time the main railhead for the battle front held by the British Army.

Quartered in the vinery

On the train to Bailleul

Knowles' Diary Continues

23rd February We arrived at Bailleul about ten miles from Ypres [in Flanders] at one o'clock. It is a small village and is teeming with munitions of war. We saw men returning from the trenches. They have six days in there at a time and four days off, and the sixth time a rest of eight complete days. Those we saw looked very exhausted. One man came straggling in without rifle or equipment and he seemed to have no idea where he was going to or what he was doing. Their eyes had a dazed look. Our battalion is quartered in a huge vinery. [*Les Grapperies du Nord*]. We have a glass covering over our heads and sleep on the earthen floor. One good thing, we were served out with waterproof sheets. It was very cold weather with slight falls of snow. We got to sleep in all our clothes with rifle and equipment at our heads, ready to move at a moment's notice. We can hear the sound of the big guns occasionally, and I have seen an aeroplane twice, now thrice.

There is a great scarcity of drinking water but any amount for washing purposes. I have lost my belt with all my money in it at Le Havre and have only a single sou left. It is rather hard lines as we can buy rolls and grapes here. Lights out at nine o'clock. A Suffolk regiment is with us here and we use the same washing place. We are fed on bully beef and biscuits principally. Our tea has no milk in it since we left Bedford but is quite good otherwise. We get soup made of bully beef and biscuits and peas - it is fearfully salty.

Wednesday 24th Feb. During the night it was fearfully cold and there was a heavy fall of snow. Reveille at 7 a.m. Our washing pipe was frozen and we had to fill our flowerpots at a dam. We have no idea what is to happen to us next. This morning we had margarine and cheese for breakfast along with tea and biscuits. A rifle inspection was held at 9 a.m. We have to wash our feet every day as long as we are here and have accommodation. In the afternoon went for a stroll around Bailleul. It is quite a large town with a beautiful townhouse dating from 1570. Behind the townhouse is a cathedral dated 1700. It is built of red bricks and has some beautiful windows of stained glass. It is less than one third the size of York Minster.

Alexander Rule

Alexander Rule, a private in U Company along with John Knowles, tells in his book *Students Under Arms* of the student soldiers visiting and admiring the *Hotel de Ville* and various old churches and houses. He described Bailleul as being at that time the centre of the lace-making industry and recounted how the students found informal drinking saloons in the kitchens of ordinary dwelling houses. There, around glowing stoves, he described how vin blanc, with hot grenadine syrup added to make it more palatable, and thin beer, helped to produce a festive atmosphere at their student sing-songs. This was in sharp contrast to his first impressions on the day of arrival in Bailleul when he wrote of the whole atmosphere of the place speaking eloquently of war, with its rain-sodden muddy streets, trench-stained troops and window frames rattling with distant gunfire.

The Diary Continues

Thursday 25th Feb. Reveille 7, breakfast 8 a.m. Rifle and feet inspection 9 a.m. Ham for breakfast, and for dinner, soup made of bully beef and biscuits and then a mixture of milk, biscuits and currants. We are to be here another night at least. Last night there was a heavy fall of snow but I was almost too warm jammed in between two others in a row of six all sleeping together. Handed in my pay book today to get it changed to sixpence a day extra instead of threepence as I am classified as a first-class shot. We can draw as much money as we want provided it does not exceed what is due, and are to be paid once a week except of course when in the trenches. We are allowed a pass outside for an hour and a half, either 11 a.m. to 12.30, or 1.30 to 3 p.m., or 3 - 4.30 p.m. I am in the third batch.

We have not yet got to our regimental headquarters which are I believe about four miles from here. Possibly we shall go there on Saturday. The British have had to retreat four miles here and the Germans are only six miles off. The nearest British gun is only one and a half miles off and we can hear firing quite near occasionally. A biplane has just flown over us not fifty yards from where I am sitting. We are very comfortable in this vinery were it not for the fearful smell that issues from a water pit not two yards from where I sleep. It is full of all sorts of refuse and must breed germs by the million. Last night we were physicked with a spoonful of lime juice. Discipline here is excellent, yet we are all hearty and in good humour.

Friday 26th February This is my birthday. [He was twenty-four years of age.] What a place to spend it. Reveille 7 a.m. Rose immediately and had a shave and wash, also knees and feet. It was a cold frosty morning and the taps being frozen I had to take a cold flowerpot with the bottom hole plugged up and fill it in the dam. My hands were nearly frozen off. Then being a mess orderly for our platoon I had just time to rush to the cookhouse and carry up a dixie of ham at 8 a.m. Feet and rifle inspection at 9 a.m. and then I spent two hours cleaning my rifle which has got very dirty. As I sat down to fill in my diary I remembered that the 26th was my birthday. This is to be no festive season it appears – I have only a mealy pudding for a birthday cake.

Yesterday as I was walking outside the town on my leave a big gun was fired and made the ground shake under me. I could also hear maxims [machine guns] spitting not far off. Had I gone a mile or two further I should have been able to see shells bursting. Met a man of the Territorial 9th London Rifles who said he had been as long as eight days in the trenches. Very few of the regular troops are now left. Territorials form the main part of the British forces and are doing wonders. The general feeling here is that the war will finish in three months. Today I am getting out from two to four. It is in orders that we are going to our Brigade headquarters tomorrow – we form part of the Second Army Corps. The British have only to hold twenty-five miles of a frontage out of a total of four hundred miles (i.e. one sixteenth of the line), but they have the best German troops against them – the Prussian Guards. We have now been a week on active service. There is little firing today as yet on account of the haze raised by the frost. Rum was served out last night but I was in bed and too lazy to get up for it.

Saturday 27th Feb. Reveille 6.30, breakfast 7.30, parade to march off at 8.30 a.m. We marched out of Bailleul to the tune of the bagpipes and the inhabitants, mostly women, turned out to see us marching past. I am not sorry to have left Bailleul, as it is a town of little interest. The only thing is the interior of the cathedral which is magnificent. Every corner is richly decorated and it has beautiful pictures on the wall, statues etc.. We marched across the Belgian frontier about two miles off and after passing through several villages came to our huts. Each hut is sixteen feet by thirty long and holds twenty-four men. The roof slopes to the very ground. It has a good corrugated iron roof, but the ends are filled in loosely with boards and mud. The floor is sunk and covered with wood. We have a waterproof sheet and blanket per man and so we are likely to be very comfortable. The guns sound terrific here – there is one just about an eighth of a mile off. We are now to take duty with our Brigade. The 1st Gordons are with us, also the Sussex and the Royal Fusiliers. We have had no hot food today except a dish of very cold tea.

Sunday 28th Feb. Spent a good night. We got a brazier going within the hut with sticks as fuel. Smoke brought tears to our eyes but it was warm and enabled us to dry our feet. The Brigadier inspected us at twelve o'clock – we are attached to the 8th Brigade of the 3rd Division of the 2nd Army Corps. Today is Sunday and we have no church of any sort and cannonading is going on as usual. It was thrilling to watch an aeroplane under German fire as the shells were bursting dangerously near it. It is a beautiful day but very cold.

Monday 1st March Reveille 6.30, physical drill and running 7.30, breakfast 8 a.m. Feet and billet inspection followed by rifle inspection and parade at 10. Fatigue work in laying road through the camp which is fearfully muddy – my part of the work was to burn tins in order to disinfect them for a foundation for the road. In the afternoon fearful clouds gathered and snow fell. At three-thirty we were inspected by General Smith-Dorrien. He is a man of good physique, rather small. His eye is bright and alert and his voice is very pleasant. News of a Prussian victory. Saw some of the 1st Gordons who came out of the trenches last night accompanied by pipe music. There are only thirty men of the original 1st Gordons left.

General Sir Horace Smith-Dorrien

Knowles' assessment of General Sir Horace Smith-Dorrien seemed to be near the mark and U Company probably already knew something of him. On 25 August 1914, in command of 2nd Army Corps, he made a stand at Le Cateau in what became the biggest battle the British Army had fought since Waterloo. The German First Army had launched a major attack on his positions, and although Smith-Dorrien managed to withdraw his troops in a skilful manner, his force of 40,000 men still suffered 8000 casualties. King George V at once sent his congratulations to Smith-Dorrien but the Commander in Chief, Field Marshal Sir John French, signally failed to do so. The general consensus of opinion amongst authorities on the Great War seems to be that Smith-Dorrien was a very competent General and that he was treated very badly by Sir John French who, with his headquarters some 30 miles or more behind the front, had decided that his troops were running away from the Germans. Alan Clark in *The Donkeys*, published in 1961, opens his book with the following exchange, which seems to sum up French's attitude to a highly intelligent commander. Sir John French: 'The British Army will give battle on the line of the Condé Canal'. Sir Horace Smith-Dorrien: 'Do you mean take the offensive, or stand on the defensive'? Sir John French: 'Don't ask questions, do as you're told'.

After the first German attack with the new weapon of chlorine gas on the French sector at Ypres on 22 April 1915 and the hasty withdrawal of the French Moroccan troops – who not unnaturally had panicked – Smith-Dorrien found himself out-flanked both on his right and left in the Ypres Salient. The Salient was simply a large bulge in the front line which meant that all the defenders, including the British troops, were exposed to enemy fire from three sides, and Smith-Dorrien's solution to the problem was to suggest on 27 April 1915 in a letter to Sir John French that the line should be straightened by withdrawing to a new line nearer to Ypres. He was at once accused by the Commander-in-Chief of being a dangerous pessimist and was relieved of his post on 6 May and sent home. He was replaced by General Sir Herbert Plumer and within days he had been authorised to carry out the withdrawal exactly as had been proposed by the disgraced Smith-Dorrien. The British Army sustained some 60,000 casualties defending Ypres where all their attacks against the Germans had to be made over flat and open ground with no cover whatsoever. Some military historians consider that with the removal of Sir Horace Smith-Dorrien the British Army lost its most able and competent General.

The Diary Continues

Tuesday 2nd March Orders as yesterday. At six p.m. A Company paraded to march off to the trenches. Col. [Thomas] Ogilvie made a speech to them mentioning three points – 1) not to speak when doing duty work, 2) not to look out at loopholes, and 3) never to leave the trench by day as German snipers use special sights.

Wednesday 3rd March Orders as yesterday but rain prevented us carrying them out. Sorry for those in the trenches as it rained continuously from 4 a.m. onwards. Our turn will come soon.

Thursday 4th March Orders as yesterday but only two hours of platoon drill from 2.15. A fatigue party of forty paraded at 8 p.m. to go out to dig trenches just behind the firing line. They were under fire for a considerable period.

Friday 5th March Orders as yesterday and I have to parade at 9.50 p.m. to go with a fatigue party to dig trenches. We have thirty rounds of ammunition in our tunic pocket but no equipment. This is to be my first experience under fire – I wonder how it feels. Some of the men who were out last night said it was rather trying. Stephen said it was the idea of physical pain alone that troubled him. Life here has been quite bearable only rather monotonous. We have shifted our lines a little higher up and now occupy the huts that belonged to A Company who are now in the trenches. The mud here is something appalling; Bedford has not a look in. We have to wash in a small burn and the banks are so soft in mud that often you sink over the ankles when washing. It is fearfully cold washing in the open early in the morning with a cold wind blowing, and after all the wash is not very satisfactory as the water is not very clean. All our drinking water has to go through the filter carts which allows one gallon per man per day. The weather is rather better but it is as cold as ever. We are stationed just beside La Clytte, a small village whose only object of interest is I believe the churchyard, where a Belgian, a French and a German officer are buried side by side. The country is very desolate and the natives that are left seem a poor harassed set of people – they all speak French.

Captain N C S Down

Shortly after this diary entry Captain Down wrote home in similar vein to his only Phyllis from the Kemmel-Vierstraat Road in support to K trenches.

But just across the road underneath the clump of trees there is always change. When first we knew the little grass clearing there were two wooden crosses in one corner. Now there must be fifty. Those two graves send a queer thrill through me whenever I see them. The older of the two crosses is bare save for the inscription.

Ci Gît
Pierre Lefroi
Mort pour la Patrie
Sept 1914

Underneath the other lies a private in the Honourable Artillery Company. Nailed to his cross is a wreath, a crown of laurel, sent out from England by his mother 'In proud remembrance'. There they lie side by side, the French poilu and the English gentleman, and who shall say whose was the greater sacrifice. We have found a garden full of primroses and planted them on some of the graves of our own men. It was the best we could do for them.

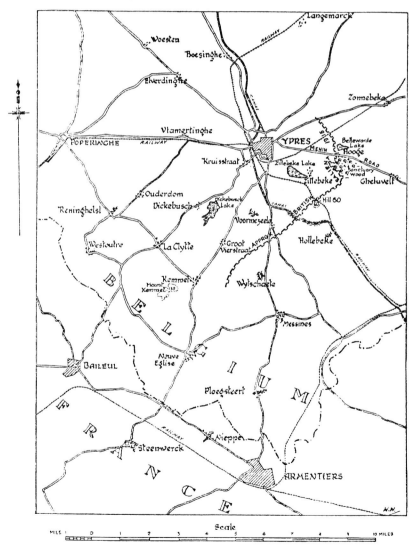

The area of U Company's activities

Down was full of praise for the Suffolks who introduced them to the nightmare that was trench warfare in Belgium in the first months of 1915. The censor's humourless blue pencil had heavily struck out the address and the first two sentences of the letter.

The War Office
Flanders

They call this farm the War Office, my dear girl, because in it you sleep all day. I wonder whose idea that was. The people who showed us how the wheels go round were an English county battalion composed chiefly of farm labourers. They were altogether topping to us. All Highlanders out here go by the name of Jocks, but these Tommies were inclined at first to refer to some of our more aristocratic privates as 'young gentlemen'. One of them was a typical Tommy of the 'Arf a mo' Kaiser' type. I never found out his name but his friends called him Woodbine and the Company Sergeant-Major referred to him as 'that bloody nuisance'. He was a weedy-looking youth and had been out since Mons. A lock of raven hair struggled out from under his cap-comforter, on the top of which his cap perched at an angle of forty-five to the vertical, the peak over the left ear. His eyes were small but twinkled and his mouth was simply great. In fact when he grinned it stretched from ear to ear. He was always singing – you could tell it was singing by the words – and he was immensely dirty. Such men are a curse back in billets but a heaven-sent blessing in the trenches.

Down's statement in his book that their programme was four days in billets followed by two days in support and two days in the firing line was also blue-pencilled out, as if morale, two years later in 1917 when the book was published, might be affected by divulging this information. Fortunately his story of sight-seeing in Ypres survived. He and a friend had gone into the town which, although half in ruins, was carrying on business more or less as usual. When they were looking through the cathedral a man in civilian clothes started to talk to them in perfect English and to question them as to the position of their battalion in the trenches. This seemed very suspicious so when they parted from him Down kept watch while his pal went to find the military police. He came back looking glum. 'They say it's only Lord Curzon' was his greeting. Still, reflected Down, they did have a good tea.

Some NCOs of the 4th Gordons at La Clytte, March 1915
Back L to R : Sgt. McKenzie, Cpl. Meldrum, Sgt. Gauld, Sgt. A Skinner, CQMS Falconer.
Front L to R : Cpl. A Crichton, Unknown, Sgt. D I Walker, Sgt. J F Fraser, Sgt. G Low, Sgt. A Allardyce.

The Diary Continues

Saturday 6th March Got off morning parade and slept or rather lay in the hut till dinner time at one. Last night I got my first taste of real work. A fatigue party of fifty men paraded at 9.50 p.m. and got fifteen sandbags and a pick and shovel each. The order was kilts, greatcoats, rifle and thirty rounds of ammunition in the tunic pocket. We had a long weary trudge of about four miles in front of us. We had been allowed no time to tie our sandbags properly together and my lot were continuously dropping off. We got into the zone of fire and marched in single file through oceans of mud. Star shells illuminated the whole country and the moon came out bright and clear. We could hear the 'zip zip' of the bullets overhead. Being night there were no shells flying but the ground was fearfully cut up with shells into holes, and I saw several 'Jack Johnsons' or holes made with the largest howitzer shell. [Howitzer shells gave off black smoke when exploding and were called after the black American boxer Jack Johnson.] We got within four hundred yards of the trenches, but just at the back of the top of the hill half way down which hid the British trenches which hang over the German lines. There we were set to make rests in a trench already dug and to fill sandbags and to drain away the water. The danger was very slight indeed, only a stray bullet could have got us, or an isolated sniper, but there was an electric thrill in hearing the sound of bullets tearing overhead. I worked at my trench as I have seldom done before. Then we got back [to the huts] by three-thirty and had hot soup waiting us.

Tonight I am on guard and have just come off my spell of two hours, six to eight p.m., in the transport field guarding the ammunition wagons. My next turn is from midnight to two a.m. guarding the cook house and the quartermaster's stores. The mud is the chief objection and I write this in the cooks hut which is also the guardroom. I can hear A Company returning from the trenches. One machine gun man has got shot through the thigh and was carried off this afternoon in the Red Cross.

After this night of trench digging U Company was paraded during the day to hear the reading of death sentences passed, and carried out, on men of other units who had been found guilty of cowardice in the face of the enemy. This exercise was repeated before their first spell in the front line trenches under the wing of the Suffolks when they were, as Rule puts it, 'entertained' to a second reading of death sentences. That this could possibly prevent any soldier from panicking in the heat of battle must have been very doubtful, and it is noteworthy that, unlike the British who shot over 300 men, the Australians did not shoot one man for cowardice, even though they took part in some of the fiercest battles of the war. This decision was taken in defiance of the British and Commonwealth forces commander-in-chief who found that there was little he could do about it.

Flanders Trenches

It is generally believed that the Great War on the Western Front was fought from trenches which ran in a straight line directly opposite one another. Both British and German trenches were built on a zigzag principle with traverses, but in the wet spring of 1915 in Belgium this was not possible. Flanders was a flat country with a high water table and little or no natural cover, and so all the trench-digging had to take place at night. The construction of effective trenches was almost impossible. Many were no more than shallow ditches about two or three feet deep, full of mud and water with a wall of sandbags piled in front of them, and these sandbags were not always proof against bullets or shell fragments. Knowles and his friends were erecting double rows of piled sandbags, built up to a height of about five or six feet above ground in front of, and behind, the short trench where they lived when in the line.

Trenches in Flanders in March of 1915 were quite unlike the continuous deep trench system dug out of the hard and unyielding white chalk of parts of France, although much better ones were dug in the dry summer weather. In Flanders the front line consisted of isolated positions about fifteen yards apart, each position holding a small number of men. Alexander Rule described them as being similar to a chain of grouse butts. James Anderson, in one of his letters home, noted that – 'Behind each wall [of sandbags], which had its own number, were anything from 6 to 12 men.' No lights or fires were allowed in them during the hours of darkness and no movement was permitted near them during the day. Because of the water, communication trenches leading up to the front line could not be constructed and so the movement of supplies, ration parties and troops over open ground was only possible at night. The sole means of communication headquarters had with the men in these trenches was by runners, and they also had to move by night. It can be imagined how very difficult it was for the men and their officers to become familiar with the layout of the trenches.

There were few barbed wire entanglements which became such a feature of later trench systems and to make matters worse there were no arrangements for cooking food, and digging latrines was impossible. The walls of sandbags, erected at night under rifle and shell fire, were frequently destroyed by German artillery and trench-mortar fire during the day and had to be laboriously reconstructed again at night. Furthermore, these sandbag breastworks had an unpleasant habit of subsiding gradually and exposing the troops to the German snipers who, using telescopic sights, were very accurate even at long range. Snipers were particularly attracted by smoke from a fire which might be lit for cooking purposes. Steel helmets, which were to prevent many head wounds, were not introduced on a large scale until the early months of 1916 and the ordinary woollen headgear or caps made the soldier's head an easy target. The Jack Johnsons were greatly feared because of the accuracy with which the mortar could be targeted and the speed with which its shells could be fired. Curiously enough, Ernst Jünger, in his book *The Storm of Steel*, published in an English translation in 1929, stated that German soldiers called shells which burst with black smoke 'Americans' or 'coal-boxes'. Rule painted a vivid picture of life in these trenches.

> Our parapet was blown in repeatedly, necessitating temporary evacuations, often in the midst of a long-deferred meal, and we would then crouch miserably for hours in a waist-deep trench; it was impossible even to kneel down, because the trench was water-logged, and so, with aching backs we had to grin and bear it. Generally we felt that the war at this stage was a bit one-sided, although we tried to maintain our offensive spirit by nightly patrols in the hope of bagging some unwary Hun for identification purposes.

At this early stage of the war U Company found that the mud and misery of the trenches was well within a day's march. Unlike the conditions of the second war, there was no motor transport for the infantry, and so they were never any great distance from the front line trenches. The danger from exploding shells was always present even in reserve billets, and U Company had little with which to sustain itself apart from the cheerful optimism of youth. It is little wonder that Knowles' diary now begins to reflect the writer's exclusive preoccupation with his personal comforts and discomforts, and the frequent danger he was exposed to of being either killed or wounded. It is not surprising that his thoughts drifted back to the life he had left in Aberdeen.

The Diary Continues

Sunday 7th March Had very little sleep and only between two and four a.m.. Was on duty from midnight until two, cold and wet, and again from six to eight - a lovely sunrise. My feet have been wet for forty-eight hours and never got my boots off. When I got off duty I was just thinking of the nice comfortable five o'clock Sunday afternoon tea I used to have - here reduced to a half cup of tea, bread and a scrape of jam.

Monday 8th March Reveille 6.30 a.m. running 7.30 a.m. breakfast. Parade 10 a.m. to get oil bottles filled. Rifle and feet inspection 12 noon, dinner 1 p.m. and parade for rations at 1.45. Very cold and snowing. Rations - slice of bully beef and cheese and loaf (petit) and four ounces of jam. This has to last no knowing how long. We paraded at 4.30 after tea and marched off about a mile to a farmhouse where we were attached to the 2nd Suffolks spread out in different sections. Law, Durward and myself are in number one section of number five platoon and we marched along about three miles to a barn close to the trenches to act as reserve. When we got there I had to go to the firing line to carry ammunition for a maxim gun. We had to keep down behind the parapet in a sort of dugout. The star shells showed up every now and then like daylight. It was rather thrilling. We are housed in the barn. Eight men killed yesterday by a shell here - two are found just behind the barn, Pte. Thain of 1st Gordons and Pte. A D Wood of 4th Gordons, the first of our battalion to be killed in action. It is quite awful to think of his being shot off almost before he realised he was under fire.

Tuesday 9th March I slept fairly well though it is a filthy, lousy place. We may be thankful to have a roof over us all the same. We had to go out at daylight and take our equipment and rifles to the back of the barn - this is in case of alarm. The artillery are firing over our heads. We are to do nothing but lie about inside all day and do fatigues at night; very risky work.

Lice and the Kilt

This reference by Knowles to a 'lousy' place is echoed by James Fraser in his diary entries for March 1915. He wrote - 'We were relieved [in the trenches] by C Company and we struggled back to Kemmel barn where we slept well in the warm straw full of lice; but were past caring'. The student soldiers had heard talk of the

THE ISSUE OF SHEEP SKIN COATS

From left to right Murdo Mackenzie, L C Scott, A Donaldson, A Crichton, R Dawson, J O Cruickshank, J M Sim, J D Pratt, A Findlater, A Gunn, Jas White, Geo Ewen, G K Saunders, J D McLaggan, James Anderson, D J Garden, C J Gordon, W R Watt.

problems of lice and had presumed that these were head and not body lice. Hence the short 'convict' haircuts which they had when in the glasshouses of the *Grapperies du Nord*. Fraser described how he searched the seams of his shirt for lice and noted that Keatings powder had little effect on them. As an experiment, he put some live lice in a tin of Keatings powder and left them for a day. He noted that they came out 'seeming livelier'.

In the Second World War, kilts were worn by soldiers only on ceremonial occasions and battle-dress was worn when marching and fighting. It is frequently forgotten that for much of the Great War all Highland battalions like the 4th Gordons wore the kilt all the time. James Fraser observed that lice not only collected in the seams of his shirt but also in the pleats of the kilt, and that out of the trenches it was a common sight to see a whole battalion de-lousing their kilts by using their thumb nails. He recounted how, when home on leave, he hung out his kilt to dry in the sun and his sister went to see how it was getting on. She returned in horror to say that the warmth had hatched out the lice which were marching up and down the pleats in column of route.

Fraser thought that the kilt was a bit of a nuisance in mud and wet as it 'fired' the back of the knees when it dried, but he was adamant that they would not have given up the kilt for anything or anybody. The ferocity of the kilted battalions in battle led to the Germans calling Highland troops 'The Ladies from Hell'.

Knowles continues his Diary

Wednesday 10th March Last night was full of excitement. I had my first real feeling of being under fire. Between nine and ten p.m. the sergeant of number five platoon called on number one section to go on fatigue duties. There were Sergeant George Low, J Durward, F W Law and myself of the Gordons and the party was completed by two of the Suffolks and a sergeant in charge. Our duty was to carry water in pig bottles to the men in the trenches - a very dangerous task.

Imagine us then, a small party of seven carrying six water bottles which weigh very heavy - four of us new to the work. Starting out from our barn we went down to the village past the place where I had been before. The road is quite straight and open and well known to the enemy. First a star shell burst and then I heard a bullet whiz over my head followed by a hurricane of shots. We have to stand stock still in close order when the star shells burst as we may be taken for clumps of brushwood. After going about five hundred yards down this slope we turned off and got into the reserve trenches. The British trenches are on the slope of the hill while the German trenches occupy the foot of the valley. All the time we could hear the 'zip zip' of the bullets. We then got orders to take the water to K2 which is the hottest trench in the line. We got out of the reserve trench and had to roll over the fifty yards interval between it and the fire trench. It was work to make your hair stand on end and in the excitement I fell over the knees in mud time and again. While in this trench, as in the last, we saw several of our company. But we had got to the wrong trench and out we went again and yet again crossing the danger zone twice instead of once as it should have been. Ill-temper saved me from being afraid. The final journey back was done quicker. These fatigue parties run more risk than those in the trenches and they are the most trying duties we have to perform. It is no use doing anything but walking on as if on a pleasure stroll; if you are hit - well it is kismet. Besides the danger of bullets there is always the risk of falling into a Jack Johnson hole as one of the other party did, and was up to the neck in water.

How thankful we are to get back safe you may imagine. I got my feet dried and went to sleep, wakening in the morning stiff in every joint. One of our field guns got into action behind us today and the Germans replied with shells which rushed through the air above our barn - we are expecting one through the roof at any time.

During the day there is little rifle fire except for snipers. We have been feeding well here one way or another. A potato plot out at the back supplies us with a dinner in addition to bully beef and ham. We can cook at a brazier and yesterday I made a jam pudding and today mashed potatoes and ham, a sort of Irish stew - very good. All the Suffolks are expert cooks of a sort. We go direct to the fire trench tonight.

March 11th Thursday Arrived in K2 trench of the firing line at eleven p.m. last night. It was very quiet on the way down without much firing. One sentry is posted in each part of the trench during the night and all are supposed to keep awake and ready. We had duty one hour out of every four. Sergeant Waters and two Suffolk men were with us two Gordons and Sergeant Low. The duty of the sentry is to look over the parapet while a star shell is up. The Germans keep firing all night just to prevent an attack. What a fearful waste of ammunition. At dawn fewer sentries are posted and the artillery commences. It is fearful the shells going whistling through the air. About four p.m. our trench was shelled with shrapnel and many of them landed not twenty yards off raising a fearful amount of earth. There is no use dwelling too much on details. The trench has a fearful smell of refuse, and dead bodies infest the air with poisonous odours. Just three yards from us was a Frenchman's foot sticking out, the rest of him covered in, to the right was a disused German trench with eighteen bodies fearfully swollen. The less one thinks about these things the better.

March 12th The night passed somehow. We have a brazier in our trench and there we can cook things. In the morning just before dawn, I had to go out of the trench behind and fill sandbags. It was a great strain on the nerves and I felt rather queer, no mistake. One of the Suffolk men fired a few grenades right on top of the German trench not two hundred yards away. About six o'clock again we were subjected to a bombardment of shrapnel and one piece of earth went down my neck. On our right was a communicating trench and at twelve noon Sergeant Jay of the 2nd Suffolks had his brains blown out by an explosive bullet. His cap went about eight feet in the air. About six-thirty I went outside the trench in front about ten yards at a listening post. I did not care very much about lying on the ground with bullets coming as close as two feet over head. We were relieved by the 1st Gordons and some of our own B Company at eight p.m. There have been two killed and one wounded in our Company, but all the original U Company have come out safe except [R M] MacTavish who has got the drum of his ear burst by the sound of a Jack Johnson. During our period in the trenches an attack was going on both on the right and the left and two hundred and seventy German prisoners were taken. Where we were, our artillery carried out a heavy bombardment of the hill as a blind. The march back was extremely tiring. We got hot soup and tea and yet had to stand by.

March 13th Breakfast at nine and rifle inspection at twelve noon. Platoon drill 2.30 and kit inspection at four - a heavy day after the trenches. We had to shave and wash, rather a job with six days growth to manipulate. We have still to stand by. There seems no doubt we are to make an effort to finish the war, only we have little chance of seeing it. I feel too wearied in mind and body to write more.

Trench Warfare

In Flanders, in early 1915, the exacting strain of trench life on troops was considerable. It was not only cold, wet and muddy but also dark for many hours. Winter nights in the front line trenches began soon after four o'clock in the afternoon and continued until about eight the next morning. Keeping awake while on sentry duty was a major problem and Alexander Rule recounted how, in the intense cold of his first dawn in the trenches, he and his friends all fell asleep and were rudely wakened by a shout of 'hands up' from a figure standing over them with a rifle. Fortunately it was not a German but a sergeant of the Suffolks out to keep his men

The

Grouse

Butts

alert, and they quickly learned a salutary lesson. Stand-to was half an hour before dawn when everyone was watchful for a possible German attack, and then there was breakfast to look forward to. Jars of tea – often laced with a little rum – had been brought up by the night ration party and a brazier was lit to heat the tea and cook the bacon. Again Rule recalled how the smoke from the brazier attracted an alert German sniper and spurts of earth thrown up by bullets flew into the tea and bacon. The daylight hours seemed as long as the night for they were quite unable to move about and became stiff, cramped and cold. U Company soon learned the dangers of stretching in the first light to relieve stiffness while crouching in a trench little more than waist high. Private James 'Gamin' Anderson, who was a fourth year honours arts student when mobilised, wrote home to his sister.

James
Anderson

1229, 16 Platoon, D Company
4th Batt.. Gordon Hghrs
Brit. Exp. Force
France
27th March

Dear Sister, (personal)

I have received all your parcels safely and must thank you for all the dainties, but the oatcakes were the best of all, nor were they broken, so they gave me the best tea I've had for a long time. But you must not send so many parcels in quick succession for I scarcely know what to do with them all. You must remember that whatever extra we wish in the trenches, these we have to carry on our backs. We cannot leave anything behind us for whenever we leave these huts, they are immediately occupied by another battalion. All goods and chattels must therefore be taken along with us. We go to the trenches tonight with barbed wire entanglements so I have no time to write.

There is very little time for correspondence here. We come out of the trenches usually for four days, but these are not idly spent. We are kept busy to keep us fit for we get no exercise in the trenches, for there you can scarcely stretch yourself without getting one of the lynx-eyed German snipers having a shot at you. You are stooping practically all the time so that exercise is essential when we come out. I can see by my father's letters that he feels it hard for me to be here and so it is. No one likes war, more especially a war like this, but duty must be done and this is undoubtedly my duty. A duty to humanity is certainly a duty to God, and if we are to be obedient to his commands, we must be prepared to sacrifice all that is nearest and dearest to us, all human affections, aye even life itself if that is necessary.

It isn't so bad out here as you would think for we care nothing for the bullets that hum about our ears or the shells that scream overhead. Backed by a good cause we are as cheery on the battlefield as in our huts, for then we have no time to think of home with all its pleasures and comforts. I do sometimes say "Oh that I were in Bonnie Scotland"!

Descriptive

'Twas Tuesday last when we set out to take our second spell of the trenches. The weather was fine and.....

[The next page of the letter is missing – almost certainly removed by the censor].

......in that position fell sound asleep. How I managed to do that I don't know for I was stiff with cold. In half an hour I was wakened for sentry duty and a jolly good job I was for I could scarcely stand on my feet, while my shoulders seemed frozen to the bone. By good luck there were too many in the trench and 14 of us had to go back. The walk was glorious. 'Tis a fine sensation to feel the warmth trickling through your feet. We went back to the same barn. The small farms about this barn, only a few hundred yards behind the firing line are all inhabited, that is, those that are left. 'Tis wonderful how these folks stuck to their homes even under shell fire. I must stop this just now for I've only 5 minutes to parade.

Goodbye and good luck, I'm off.
Your loving brother
Jimmie

The Diary Continues

March 14th Sunday Went sick as I was not very well. There was church parade which I am sorry I missed as I believe the chaplain was very good. A heavy bombardment is going on [at St Eloi on their left flank] and we have to sleep with our clothes and boots on.

March 15th Monday Parade for company drill at 9 a.m. We had hot baths in the afternoon, each platoon going off in succession. A house in La Clytte is fitted up with a boiler and tubs. Two men in a tub and a bucket of dirty water is taken out and a bucket of clean water substituted after each platoon. There was plenty of disinfectant in the water otherwise it would not be safe. It was quite a treat to get clean again. The move is off and we shall get a chance of a good sleep with boots off which I have not had since before being in the trenches

16th March Tuesday Running and physical drill at 7.30 and platoon drill and relay race 10-12.15. Marched off to the trenches at 7.45 p.m. We passed through Kemmel three miles off and then went to K trenches. Our section was in K4 in a line of about thirty-five yards. There were sixteen of us including Lt [James I] Watson. The night passed uneventfully except for the energy of a particular sniper who made us careful. Scarcely had the day fully dawned when L C Scott got shot through the head while stretching himself. He expired with a sigh, his equipment dyed with blood. This made us all very quiet and sober. We were relieved at seven-thirty and a stretcher party arrived and took up the body. It was slow going with the stretcher. I had four turns of carrying it myself and it is wondrous how heavy a dead body is. The face also was uncovered and made me chary of looking over my shoulder when in front. Poor Scott, I knew him well after we got to Bedford. He was in my own year in New College, Edinburgh, and only twenty-two years of age, full of the salt of life. It is awful to think how war cuts off so many in the flower of life. Yet he died well and practically without pain. I feel sorry for his people. He is buried at Kemmel. We went five hundred yards to a farm house and our section slept in a shed along with two calves. There was a roof but only part of a wall, and straw and rotten potatoes on the floor.

Membership of U Company

Membership of U Company was not restricted entirely to students and graduates of the University of Aberdeen. Lance-Corporal L C Scott was an arts graduate of the University of Edinburgh and a divinity student when he joined the Lothian and Border Horse at the outbreak of war. He managed to get himself transferred to U Company in Bedford and accompanied them to France in February. He was the first member of U Company to be killed. Sergeant James Fraser recorded in his diary that after stand-to at 6 am on 17 March for the usual half hour, they did a foolish thing by firing rifles at the German trenches to wake them up a bit, and, as a direct result of that, Scott was killed. A very subdued section kept well under cover for the rest of the day. In these early days the Gordons carried their dead comrades considerable distances from the trenches to give them a Christian burial. As the fighting increased in intensity they buried them where they were killed, if at all possible.

One month after Scott's death another Edinburgh member of U Company, Private J M S (Stewart) Paterson, was killed by a sniper's bullet near Ypres on 22 April 1915. Paterson, a former pupil of Robert Gordon's College in Aberdeen, was also an honours arts graduate of Edinburgh and had never been a student at Aberdeen,

James F Fraser as an officer in the Seaforths

but he had formed so many friendships with Aberdeen students that he became a member of U Company before the war and went with them to Bedford and then to France. Corporal George McSween of U Company is another whose name does not appear in Mabel Allardyce's *University of Aberdeen Roll of Service in The Great War* which was published in 1921. McSween was a student at Aberdeen Training Centre when he joined his friends in U Company and was killed in an attack on Y Wood, just north of the Menin Road, on 16 June 1915 at the age of 23. A long communication trench which U company helped to dig for this battle was named 'Union Street' after the main street in Aberdeen. After the war, the 'Union Street Graveyards' No's 1 and 2, which contained the graves of men who fell in August and September 1915, were incorporated in the military cemetery at Zillebeke.

The Diary Continues

18th March Thursday I slept well through sheer exhaustion. The worst thing about this life is want of sleep. You get too tired even to mind the bullets. My feet were cold lying practically outside an opening. The two calves have the most comfortable part. In the morning we started a great scene of alfresco cooking. First tea, then pea soup and potatoes, and finally chocolate cakes ground down. [On this date James Pratt ceased to be the Company Sergeant-Major and was promoted to the rank of 2nd Lieutenant in his own Battalion. The popular Sergeant George Low, who had been with the Company since 1910, now became CSM].

19th March Friday Passed sleepless night - feet too cold. Nothing to do all day but eat and dig a sentry pit and also fatigues. A severe snowstorm came on and covered us up in our shed. About 2 a.m., after being chilled to the heart, Captain Mackinnon had pity on us and let us crowd inside with the officers' servants and the sick. Here I was unfortunate enough to lie down in the draught of the door which swung a clear six miles off the floor, so I got no sleep for cold. Usual 'drumming up' and eating throughout the day. We are becoming expert cooks and are not over careful in experimenting with our stomachs. We left for the trenches at 7.30 p.m. It was a moonlight night and we had to be very careful. We got to the trench called K2 - to the left of where I had been before. It was fearfully muddy but all right if you kept to the planks laid down; but this was impossible in a strange place at night.

20th March Saturday Last night was a heavy fall of snow. For hours I sat shivering in an open trench with nothing but a waterproof sheet over my head. I am sorry I left my woolly hat at La Clytte. During the day it got warmer but we were too crowded to get stretched out for a sleep.

21st March Sunday Last night was warmer but I was done up for want of sleep. We had to work filling sandbags during our two hours of sentry-go, so that I had to get into the shelter and fell asleep utterly exhausted. It is a beautiful day but awful to think it is Sunday. We get relieved tomorrow night if all goes well making three clear days in the trenches. In fact we should have been as well off in the trenches for the whole six days.

22nd March Monday Still in the trenches. No drinking water to be had and very little for boiling. We were relieved by C Company about 10.30 p.m. and had a very quiet exit. The moon was almost half full and enabled us to avoid the Jack Johnson holes and get a dry road.

23rd March Tuesday Had a splendid sleep till 8.30 a.m. Went out and had a cup of coffee at a little croft for a penny, also a loaf for eight pence. At two-thirty we had to turn out and go into dugouts at the roadside. No fires allowed in the barn now as C Company got shelled yesterday afternoon. The shells are flying to our right and rain is beginning to fall.

24th March Wednesday We came back to billets at La Clytte last night. Today there is the usual cleaning up - very tiresome.

25th March Thursday Reveille 6.30, breakfast 8, parade 9.30. Parade 6.30 p.m. to carry barbed wire entanglements to reserve barn about four miles off where A and B Companies are. Got back dead beat at 12.30 with wet feet.

26th March Friday Light duty at company office. Next we go into the trenches as a battalion. Military life is apt to break a man's spirit. It is petty when away from the actual fighting. Most of us are happier in the trenches than out of them.

27th March Saturday Got a day's detention with sore throat. Battalion office at 9 a.m. - four days CB [Confined to Barracks]. Military discipline destroys individuality outwardly but cannot quench the spirit.

28th March Sunday Church parade 11 a.m. - 'A man shall be as the shadow of a rock in a weary land'. Close order drill at 2.30. Four mile walk with fatigue party to reserve trench at 6.30 with barbed wire.

On this day John Knowles wrote to his friend John McConachie in Aberdeen.

28/3/1915

My Dear John,

I have received your cheery letter which is more welcome to me than you can have any idea of. The cigars you sent were like a whiff of old times when we smoked together those which Pat [Peter McConachie] brought back from Las Palmas. To me they seem very old times indeed, though not so very long ago measured by the time since our friendship began. Out here we appreciate friends at home and I think I can count you about my closest - eh, old chap? I don't think you should bother about enlisting as I do not think you would stand the life out here. It requires a much better digestion than Providence has blessed you with to stand the kind of food we get here. Of course it is quite good and nourishing but somehow or other nearly everybody is suffering from some bowel complaint - your humble servant included, though I am not so bad.

I have now been six days in the trenches altogether and five in the reserve, which is equally dangerous though one does not feel it so much. Life in the trenches is not so bad as we thought. The hardest thing we have to endure is want of sleep as we have sentry duty one out of every three hours at night and one out of six or five or three during the day as it happens. Officers and Non Coms do not feel this so much as they have no sentry duty and can get at least one good sleep every day, so they don't quite know what the men have to endure. All the firing and relief and fatigue work falls due at night and this is when we have to keep awake. All the firework displays I have ever seen are cast into the shade by the displays of star shells that go on almost continuously during the night. The weather has been good here except for a little snow, and a few days ago heavy rain. It has been cold and frosty today but beautiful and clear overhead. We are lucky to be in huts now which are the most comfortable dwellings we have.

Would you mind sending me one of those copying ink pencils with the steel protectors, also a scribbling book with plain hard paper for writing a personal diary? I have seen them in your office. Envelopes also are scarce here and not to be bought. However don't hurry or bother yourself about it.

Kindest regards,
Ever your pal
John F Knowles

The Diary Continues

29th March Monday Parade to N9 trenches at 6.30. In reserve, seven hundred yards from the Germans, very comfortable with plenty of water to boil.

30th March Tuesday Relieved at 7.30. Went to farm about 1100 yards from Germans on skyline. Waterproof sheets over the door and enter from behind so as not to show a light. All fires to be lit at night. If they go out in daytime not to be lighted again. Fatigue to the firing line with gangways. Very difficult to carry. Trench digging at side of barn up to three a.m. Stand to 4.15 till after 5 a.m. Waterproof sheets taken off doors and we wait till daylight in full marching order.

31st March Wednesday Lay about in the barn all day squeezed into a cattle stall with F W Law. Managed to snooze intermittently. Plenty to eat but not allowed outside the door. After dark, fatigue party to fire trench N7 with barbed wire entanglements. Again fatigue with rations to N9, our old trench. After that, digging a trench at side of barn from two to three a.m. We are making day into night and the reverse.

1st April Thursday Slept forenoon and wrote afternoon in barn. At dusk had two fatigues – went to the cross-roads behind for rations, then set off in full equipment for trench M3 carrying a bag of 'Maconochies'. [Maconochie – named after the packer – was a tinned ration of chopped meat with carrots, onions, beans and potatoes, and provided a satisfying meal when heated.]

2nd April. Good Friday Passed the night in the trench in fatigue and sentry duty – no sleep, two hours on and one hour rest, usually less. Firing quiet and very cold towards dawn. Beautiful day, birds singing, lovely country, yet here and there the fair scene is marred by dead bodies of man and beast lying around giving off a pestilential vapour. Even as I write I lift my head and see fourteen dead cattle and two Frenchmen lying about a hundred yards behind our trench. In front and to the right not more than a hundred yards off is the German trench, in the centre and to the left it is further away. This is the best trench I have been in so far as it is new and built at leisure. We are busy all night making improvements. Every one of us is longing for the war to end. The horror of it all is too great to dwell on. Yet we have not been in an engagement yet, but the sights of previous attacks abound, e.g. the wood at Wytschaete where the 1st Gordons made their gallant but futile charge. Our casualty list in the 4th is mounting up – an officer's servant was killed in N9 yesterday.

Saturday 3rd April Wet, cold night and drizzle all day.

Sunday Easter Dull morning then gradually cleared up. Read Revelations chapters 1-5, John 20-21. The clearing up of the weather on Easter was like the dawn of the Resurrection after the dullness of the Crucifixion.

Monday 5th Relieved last night and got back to La Clytte. Met several of the reserve draft I knew – they have been on active service since a week past Thursday. Rain kept us off parade and we had rifle inspection at 4.30 within the huts.

Tuesday 6th April Reveille 6.30 a.m. Running and rapid marching 7.30, breakfast 8 a.m. rifle inspection 9.30, hut inspection, platoon drill 10-12 noon, bathing parade 12.30, late dinner 2 p.m. Parade for relay races 3 p.m. Finish about 4.30 with tea. This gives an idea of how we are kept busy when out of the trenches. The exercise is necessary in order to get rid of the trench stiffness. It has been a fine day, though cold, but now it is pouring rain like yesterday.

Wednesday and Thursday 7th and 8th As usual. No afternoon parade as we proceed to the trenches.

Sunday 11th April Spent in reserve barn outside Kemmel. Last night slept with my back opposite a hole and got a chill. During the daytime aeroplanes were very numerous, also a battery of our big guns kept firing over us making a deafening roar. Weather beautiful.

Monday 12th Last night was beautiful starlit. Went to K2B trench carrying two bottles of water. Also to L1 (which is a reserve trench) with barbed wire entanglements ten feet long and two and a half feet high. During the afternoon we had the excitement of watching aeroplanes being shelled– very few I believe are ever damaged in this way.

Tuesday 13th Last night went up to see the doctor from barn. Temp. 101 – was sent to hospital in La Clytte. Spent comfortable night in warm room with brazier. Sent down in motor to Westoutre and then to ward No 1.

Wednesday 14th Spent comfortable night and had good food.

Thursday 15th Porridge for breakfast. Sent off after dinner to ward No 4 as convalescent. It is on the outskirts of Westoutre and stands high on a slight hill. The building is of red brick and has a tiled roof. It is a nunnery and still occupied by nuns. The wards are in an attic up a wooden ladder or stair. The red tiles of the roof are all we have to cover our heads but they are in good repair and there are plenty of small windows. A long table occupies the centre of each part with forms and a lamp overhead. We have our meals at the table and can play games and read. We sleep on mattresses on the floor and have three blankets each and a pillow.

Sunday 18th April Last night a heavy bombardment going on towards St Eloi and Ypres. Something is in the air. [What was in the air was the first gas attack of the war by the Germans on April 22nd in the north of the Ypres salient]. To-night attended a short open air Anglican service. Aeroplanes hovering all round. Visited the cathedral of Westoutre. It is fairly roomy and profuse in decorations, inclined to become gaudy.

Monday 19th Beautiful sunshine continues. Went for a walk and met some 9th Lancers. Spoke to one and he said they were exercising the horses ready for an advance.

Sunday 25th April Discharged hospital. Walked back to La Clytte.

This is the last entry in the diary. John Knowles rejoined U Company on 4 May. He was killed by the bullets of a German sniper to the head and chest whilst digging a communication trench some two hundred yards from the enemy lines near Ypres on 5 May 1915 and was buried in a small farmyard at Kemmel in what was then known as the Gordon cemetery. He was laid to rest on 6 May by his friends in U Company, with his fellow divinity student J K Forbes reading the burial service. Sandy Rule faithfully recorded the event in his diary and noted that the little cemetery was growing. John Knowles now lies in the cemetery at Wytschaete in Belgium along with other members of U Company.

The cemetery at Wytschaete

CHAPTER FIVE

Soldiering On

JOHN Knowles died in May of 1915. The other members of U Company soldiered on, burying their dead while not forgetting them, and not yet fully aware of what yet lay ahead of them in the following months. From their surviving diaries it is clear that many members of the Company wrote careful letters of sympathy to the parents of those students and graduates who had been killed. Nevertheless, with the cheerful optimism of youth, and in spite of their losses, they continued to sing as they had done since their Bedford training as they marched to and from the trenches. Their repertoire was considerable and consisted of musical hall ditties of the day along with old favourites from the *Students' Song Book*, although they were just as likely to be singing *The Soldiers' Chorus* from *Faust*. Not that they were averse to the more earthy and ribald versions of soldiers' songs, and when they were in Bedford, Colonel Ogilvie forbade them to sing when marching through villages lest they upset the inhabitants with some of their words. Their late Sergeant-Major Bewick, who was a freemason and a religious man, had become almost apoplectic when they bawled out the following words to the tune of the mission hymn, *What a Friend we have in Jesus.*

> *When this bloody war is over,*
> *No more soldiering for me.*
> *When I get my civvie clothes on,*
> *Oh, how happy I shall be!*
>
> *No more church parades on Sunday,*
> *No more asking for a pass,*
> *I shall tell the Sergeant-Major*
> *To stick his passes up his arse.*

There was no transport of any sort for U Company and the mud and misery of the trenches was never more than a few hours march away from their supposedly safe billets. They confided to their diaries that the songs they sung when on the march not only helped to lift their spirits, but also seemed to shorten the journey when their steps were flagging, and they paid little attention to *Alma Mater's* carping that *Tipperary* seemed to have replaced the National Anthem in their affections. They sang unless they were unbearably tired or the death of a popular member of the Company had occurred. 'No more *Maid of Morven* in Sandy's fine tenor voice', Alexander Rule wrote in his diary on the day after Sergeant Sandy Skinner and Private Stewart Paterson had been killed by snipers' bullets. When Private David Crichton was killed on a fatigue party two days after the death of John Knowles on 5 May, the diary entry read – 'another bright spirit gone west'.

Towards the end of May 1915 news filtered through of the Gallipoli landings, and U Company had a personal interest in the casualty list, for among the missing there was a familiar name. This was Hector Guthrie, another of the former pupils of the renowned – certainly in the north-east of Scotland - Fordyce Academy, at least 12 of whose former pupils were members of U Company. Guthrie entered the University of Aberdeen as second bursar in the winter of 1910 when he joined U Company. As a sergeant in the Company at the outbreak of war, Guthrie - who had a first-class honours degree in English - went to Bedford with the 4th Gordons for training. Anxious to increase his chances of being sent to the front early in the war, he applied for and obtained a regular commission in the Lancashire Fusiliers. It was later confirmed that he had been killed at Gallipoli. The fact that the war now appeared to have become static on the Western Front suggested to the members of U Company that the Germans had been forced to a standstill through exhaustion. There were no real grounds for that optimism but there was a strong feeling that a big breakthrough was being planned by the Allies and that the war would soon be brought to a successful conclusion.

Static Warfare

A J P Taylor in *The First World War* (1963), stated that Lord Kitchener, the Secretary of State for War, 'with one of his gleams of insight', wrote to Sir John French as early as January 1915 to the effect that it had to be recognised that the French Army could not make a sufficient break through the German lines of defence to bring about a German retreat from northern France. The German lines could neither be carried by a direct assault nor completely invested. Kitchener appeared to be almost alone in this view so early in the war, and all the training of British troops was aimed at making use of their enthusiasm for the war and their zeal to finish it by the method of direct frontal assaults on the German lines, no matter how strongly they were held.

The tactics adopted of attacking the German trenches with troops advancing over open country in line abreast and each man a few paces from his neighbour were to continue for much of the war. It was still hoped for many months that the enemy line could be broken sufficiently for the cavalry to sweep through and around the Germans. There was to be very little change in these tactics until the Germans themselves launched a major offensive on 21 March 1918 with dramatic results. They had managed to assemble a large attacking force by moving men at night, and the long advancing lines of men were replaced by well-armed mobile groups looking for the weakest points to break through. Allied to that they attacked, not by night, but with the aid of a thick fog which was more by good luck than by design.

Hill 60 and The Salient

Early in May 1915 U Company left Kemmel and were sent to Hill 60. A few miles away, at Langemarck, the Germans had carried out one of the earliest gas attacks of the war on 22 April with devastating effects. Alexander Rule duly recorded the attack and continued:-

> Our Corps Commander gave us an inspiring talk. We were booked for Hill 60 and we were to hang on to it at all costs, poison gas or no poison gas. Our gas masks at this time, incidentally, consisted of a piece of cotton waste soaked in chemicals, and precious moments were used up in teasing this out sufficiently to protect the nose and mouth. The Germans, failing to drive us off the top with gas, might attempt to 'blow us up with mines' - but as Highlanders we were expected to hang on with our proverbial dourness.

In the end of the day chemical warfare proved to be a disappointment, although on both sides there were high hopes of a speedy end to the war through its use. Chlorine discharged from cylinders against French colonial troops was the gas used by the Germans in April 1915 to world-wide condemnation, disposing of the idea, which was finally laid to rest at Hiroshima, that war was either noble or chivalrous.

The Battalion spent eight days in the trenches at Hill 60 in wet and muddy conditions – it rained continuously – amidst the corpses of many of the unburied dead of both sides, and under constant bombardment by shell-fire. Rule recounted how Sergeant James Morrison, the third year medical student, when out with a fatigue party, gave a spontaneous organ recital in a roofless church at the village of Zillebeke within a kilometre of the front line, and how they all rushed for cover in case the organist aroused the wrath of the Germans. After eight days, on 20 May, U Company left Hill 60 for rest billets at Rozenhill near La Clytte, but fresh fighting broke out in the Salient and they soon found themselves marching through the silent ruins of Ypres on their way to and from the trenches near the Menin Road. Rule recalled one such occasion when, trudging silently through the eerie quiet of the shelled city, they came upon the walls of the 'English Ladies'

Sergeant James Morrison

Seminary'. On the instant, someone whistled wistfully the opening bars of *Gaudeamus*, which in other days would have brought the bajanellas to the windows of their digs in the Rosemount district of Aberdeen. A sudden laugh from the Company's ranks showed that thoughts of home had not been far away.

Alma Mater

Back home in Aberdeen *Alma Mater* carried occasional articles from members of U Company in France. In June 1915 they published an account of the Company's adventures from the pen of Private Douglas McLean from Boddam, near Peterhead, who was a third year arts student serving his fourth year with U Company.

Home Thoughts From Abroad

April, April, laugh thy girlish laughter;
Then, a moment after, weep thy girlish tears.

I have often wondered why Chaucer made April of the firmer sex, or worse still, neuter. Surely nothing was ever more feminine, more mobile, more undependable, than this weather we're trying to enjoy. Yet it is typical of our life and temperament out here, optimism glimpsing through by sheer force when we have come to the conclusion that the whole thing is a 'pure wash-out', military life a farce, and life a question – or exclamation – mark.

Well, here we are, seasoned veterans, war-worn soldiers, modest heroes in embryo. Bedford is a pleasant dream, a jumble of delightful memories, a part of the past to recall and have heartache over. The leaving was hard, though the change took off the edge. All the rest, the train journey with the funny sensation in our spines at the sight of the loaded ambulance trains; the sea voyage with the glamour of the moon on searchlight-swept waters, the long up-hill march at Havre, the wee boys eluding the police and chattering bewilderingly in our tents; the long journey in literal horse-boxes (*hommes* 40; *chevaux* 8), the roundhead 'crops' in the glasshouse, the baptism of fire, so disappointing in sensation, the rain, snow, sunshine, spelling holidays or work; strange that all half fade and that the half we keep is besmeared with beauty. Always the past, the past!

The Company has become curiously consolidated in temper and ideals. It has become a whole-hearted 'grouser', as a good Company should, and it has at last taken soldiering at least half seriously. I don't think it will ever go further, in spite of strenuous efforts on the part of misguided authority. It persists in refusing to climb or descend to the level of the true 'swaddie'. Certainly it can never aspire to the joviality and unfailing good spirits of the English 'Tommy', but that is because it is Scotch and can't talk enough to forget everything in words.

We have suffered some changes, including the hero of many of our Bedford notes, who has taken his Majesty's commission and is thereby comparatively immune from our scathing remarks. Also, strictly speaking, the Company is defunct. Its dignity has shrunk to a paltry couple of platoons - ichabod! The choice of Low as Company Sergeant-Major is one of the few events which have been awarded a growl of assent since we came out.

We are billeted in huts, twenty to a hut, and naturally *cliques* are formed, insomuch that we sometimes wonder if so-and-so (two huts up) is here or at home. The development of character we wonder at is perhaps only another instance of good being latent in everyone. Certainly the Company has been very fortunate in recent 'discoveries of the war'. By 'good', tender Bajan, we don't mean 'goodyness', the development we speak of is along the lines of cheek, camaraderie, and arrogant optimism. McLennan and 'Buchie's' sole representatives are absolutely indomitable and irrepressible. We sometimes wonder, as we wander 'home' dog-tired from a week in the trenches, whether the laugh extorted from us when we thought to laugh no more is more annoying or delightful, but 'Buchie's' ribaldry or McLennan's 'Tidilley-i' generally recalls the pride of race; we totter on, over execrable roads, and I believe we are grateful for their exertions.

Our casualties have been few, comparatively, though it was a shock to realise that any of us could really be hit. Bullets that come from nowhere don't seem to play the game somehow, and it's a sneaking kind of warfare to hustle into trenches and wait for 'Jack Johnsons' or a stray pellet! In the trenches we have to cook our own grub; I wish some of you could come and see the zest with which we devour the results of our efforts!

Yet in spite of the prosaic nature of it all, there are moments of pure poetry. The country is lovely still, and spring is in our veins through all the woeful sordidness. When that fails, the longing for peace and home gives us sensations to which we were hitherto comparative strangers. Some of our cynical friends fear that we shall be serious when we get back to King's. Who knows?

We don't know whether there will be a second summer number of *Alma*; if not, we must 'breathe a fond farewell' to those who have drunk their cup a round before. When we come back there will be a new race of Tertians, and we'll have to carve a niche in unknown granite. However, good luck to you all, you who are leaving orthodox-wise the scene whither our fancy roams - *bon voyage et bon chance*!

Before the Great War all students at King's College in Aberdeen were named according to their sex, and the year they were in. First year students were 'bajans' and 'bajanellas', second year students were 'semis' and 'semilinas', third year students were 'tertians' and 'tertianas' and fourth year honours students had the grand title of 'magistrands'. First year medical students at Marischal College had an apposite title – they were known as 'lambs'.

The Ypres Salient

U Company was about to undergo one of its worst and longest spells in the trenches which lasted from 26 May until 19 June, before once more retiring for rest and further training at Brandhoek near Vlamertinghe. The trenches they were sent to occupy near the village of Hooge were in the tip of the Ypres Salient and Rule describes the Very lights at night soaring in all directions, both front and rear – or so it appeared – and how they were at a loss to know where exactly the German positions lay, and felt as if they were completely surrounded.

The effortlessly fluent pen of Captain Down in his letters home reinforced Rule's remarks about the impression of being surrounded when serving in the front line of the Ypres Salient.

From the letter of June 2nd 1915.

At last we reached the outskirts of Ypres. At the bridge where the sentry stands, guarding the ruined city from the hand of the looter, the pipers turned aside and broke into *Hielan Laddie*. From the men came what a journalist would probably describe as a 'deep-throated roar' and for the life of me I can't give a better word for it. In it blended the voices of the businessmen, students, clerks, artisans, farm labourers, stevedores and all the other classes which go to make up the battalion. As we entered Wipers it died down, for who could be aught but silent in that city of the dead. Past the Cloth Hall, past the cathedral, past shops and houses now little heaps of crumbling brick, through the Menin Gate, across the moat and out into the Salient. And you can't understand what that word means, Phyllis, until you have stood as we have stood, on Hill 60 or up at Hooge, and seen the sky on all sides of you lit up by German flares, or until you have seen your *own* men hit in the back with shrapnel when they were facing the enemy. Take a map and you will see that the Germans are on three sides of you only, but watch the lights by night and nothing will persuade you that they are not all round.

The men we relieved had been cut up even worse than the Hill 60 lot, and as they had been driven back by the gas, we found ourselves taking over open positions behind hedges instead of trenches. Our men of course, were dead fagged by the time they got there but we had to set them to dig themselves in without a moment's rest. Poor devils. But at dawn we were so far down that the Hun had only our head and shoulders to pot at instead of our entire weary anatomies. Since then we have spent the time being shelled by their artillery – yesterday we had thirteen hours of it without a moment's respite. By night we try to rebuild the trenches which have been blown in by day. After the Germans have been shelling us for an hour or so our own artillery will reply with one round of shrapnel, generally a 'dud'. If only the BEF could lay hands on the man whose fault it is, he would have a pretty rough crossing.

Was out in No Man's Land last night firing rifle grenades. It was creepy work out there in the long wet grass in which you kept running against dead bodies. To my dismay all the grenades failed to explode, and it was not till we got back safely that I remembered I had not pulled out the pins! And at a guinea a time that's hardly helping to win the war is it? We hear (1) that our depleted battalion is shortly to return home to recruit, (2) that all Territorial Force battalions are to be withdrawn from the firing line, (3) that we are to do an attack, (4) that we are to form the nucleus of a new conscript battalion and (5) that we are going to Rouen to dig drains. There's a fine selection for you. Take your choice and it's certain to be untrue. Meanwhile here we are stretched across the road to Ypres and holding what is probably the most important part of the whole line.

With which cheery thought, farewell.

Your

Tired Thomas

Some of the horrors U Company and the 4th Gordons experienced were conveyed realistically by Down in his letters, but he managed always to mitigate the harshness of the situation as his sense of humour kept breaking through with some of his more improbable stories. Perhaps the very writing of the letters served to keep up his own morale as well as that of his audience at home.

Same place
June 12th

Cherie (French),

Still here and no word of being relieved. That's only nineteen days that we've been in the front line without a relief, and we haven't lost more than two hundred men during that time so we aren't doing so badly. All the same, life's hardly worth living. From dewy dawn till the stars begin to peep the Hun shells us, shell after shell the whole day long and we just have to sit and look pleasant. Our own artillery do their best but all they can do is to polish their guns and think how nice it would be to have something to fire out of them. If only we could have the man here who said that there was no shortage of shells.

I'm not being very cheerful, am I, but at present I'm suffering rather badly from lack of sleep. This morning after 'stand to' I told my servant to make me a cup of cocoa. Before it was ready I had fallen asleep and he had to wake me. I took the cocoa from him and tried to drink it but it was too hot and so I sat down and waited for it to cool. I must have fallen off again directly as I woke up with a start to find scalding liquid trickling down my kilt and on to my bare knees. I didn't want my man to see what a fool I had made of myself, so I raked up an old Tommy's cooker and put a dixie of water on it. My dug-out was on fire when I woke up again and I had to use all my remaining water to put it out. After this I gave up all idea of a hot drink and went to sleep on the sopping floor of the dug-out. Five or six hours later a small earthquake roused me to the fact that all around me was dark. This was astonishing for a midday in June. A shell had closed the dug-out door, an ungentlemanly thing to do, but perhaps better than coming in through the door. When my men dug me out they told me that this sort of thing had been going on for over an hour, and that they had retired to the far end of the trench, and had wondered why I didn't do likewise.

The Battle for Y Wood

In June U Company took part in another small battle – described by Rule as a fight, on one of June's most perfect days, for the possession of a miserable copse in Flanders. Today it is known as the first attack on Bellewaarde, between the Menin Road and the railway, and it took place on 16 June 1915. Here the Company's casualties began to mount, although James Anderson, the arts student from Portknockie, and Lance-Corporal Sandy Gunn, the big medical student from Caithness and a well-known University athlete, both had narrow escapes when carrying messages back over open ground swept by shell and machine-gun fire. Gunn was mentioned in dispatches for surviving three such hazardous journeys and Anderson was commended by Colonel Ogilvie. Corporals Murdo MacIver and George McSween were both hit in the head and killed during the attack, and ten others wounded.

U Company's casualties now numbered about 15 men wounded, some of them more than once, and six killed, so they were pleased to see four of their wounded back from hospital in Rouen. On the day they returned to the Roll an unlucky shell killed two of them and wounded the other two. Captain Lachlan Mackinnon had now gone home and the new commanding officer was Captain J G (Hoppy) Hopkinson. He was joined by two new platoon commanders who had arrived with a draft of officers – one of them was 2nd Lieutenant Walter Inkster, a graduate of Aberdeen in arts and science; the other was 2nd Lieutenant W J C Sangster, MA, a medical student and an old U Company member. The 25 year-old Walter (Wattie) Inkster, who curiously enough had worked for the German Potash Syndicate in 1913, had given up a good agricultural appointment in Australia to return to Scotland and join the 4th Gordons as a private in March of 1915. He received a commission in April and crossed to France in May and joined U Company.

Captain Down's company of the 4th Gordons was in support in this action at Bellewaarde and he described the fighting as he saw it from the trenches.

Still the same spot
June 18th

This is a great life, Phyllis, if it wasn't for the death. We have been in our first show, and for the last twenty-four hours have been shaking hands with ourselves at still being in the land of the living. I had a good look at myself this morning in my steel pocket mirror but failed to find any grey hairs or fresh furrows of care across my forehead. That wasn't surprising though, as the mirror has become so rusty that it takes some time to find out what part of your face is being reflected in it.

You will probably have read by now that our line was advanced along the Menin Road on a front of so much and on a depth of so much. This advance will no doubt be heralded as a fresh victory, but.... Oh, all right, Mister Censor, I won't if you don't want me to. Our battalion was not in the charge but was holding the trenches from which it was made. It was just as well, as the men could hardly be described as in the best of health after twenty-three days in the front line without a really healthy drink all the time. The water that comes up to us every night is a sickly brown, doped with chlorate of lime to kill the weaker microbes. Anyhow we got it in the neck a bit, as the Germans shelled us hard the whole time the show was going on, and one company [U Company] had to go up and consolidate the captured line, and lost a bit on the way up.

The attack was made at dawn and was heralded by the first real bombardment got up by our guns. For half an hour the shells were just tumbling over each other in a wild rush to get to the German trenches, and then one of the other brigades in the division went over the top. As they went our men stood on the parapet and cheered them on. It was a great sight and you quite forgot to notice that the shells were falling round you too. An eight-inch crump descended on our trench and hit the parapet, covering the veteran of the platoon with earth, but failing to explode. Which was just as well for all concerned, as an eight-inch crump is no laughing matter. The veteran picked himself and indulged in a selection from those expressions so dear to the heart of the 'old soldier'. When he had finished his face lit up with a grin. 'Eh, but I can dee wi' a seat fine', and he sat himself down calmly on the dud and went on looking at the attacking line, which we could just see clambering into the first line of German trenches.

84

A few minutes later, as we were all talking excitedly in our trench, one of the sentries cried out 'Here come the Gairmans', and when I jumped up on to the fire step to have a look, there they were advancing in a mass towards us. By now all the men were manning the parapet waiting for the order to fire, which I was keeping back until the Huns were right up to the wire. Suddenly I noticed something about them. They were unarmed. Then it struck me that they must be prisoners, but there was no sign of any guard. Down the road they came in fours running to beat the wind, evidently wanting to get away from the nasty war as soon as possible. At least a hundred yards behind them came their guard, one man in full equipment with a rifle on which was fixed a red-tipped bayonet, and on his head a German helmet. Weighed down by his arms and booty he was utterly unable to keep up with his charges, and as he passed us was steadily losing ground. You should have heard him puffing by, anathematising breathlessly the over-eagerness of his flock. We sank into the bottom of the trench and shook with laughter for five minutes. I don't mind if I never see a more amusing sight. One of the men as he passed waved his hand to us and shouted in English – 'Back to good old Lunton'.

The following story is guaranteed by my platoon sergeant. I have known more truthful men than he is apt to be when facts look like spoiling fiction. Up in the trenches there was one spot only about fifteen yards from the Hun, and here some of the leading humorists of the platoon used to foregather of a morning to indulge in badinage with similarly minded Huns across the way. One day the sanitary man – a very witty fellow I am led to believe – had a brainwave. After a certain amount of wordy warfare he adopted a more serious tone, and informed the Germans that they must behave well on the morrow as certain members of the Cabinet were to make a tour of the trenches. Next day the humorists proceeded along the trench bearing on the end of sticks a variegated collection of headgear boned from Ypres; top hats, bowlers and the more humble felt hat. As they went they hurrahed loudly, with the intention of making the Hun think that the Ministers were being shown around. To their disappointment nothing happened. They had expected at the very least showers of bombs (some people have a remarkable sense of humour), shells, and perhaps with luck the 'Hymn of Hate'. But nothing happened. After the demonstrations were over the incensed sanitary man got into conversation with his friends the enemy and asked them if they hadn't noticed the Cabinet going round. Yes, they had spotted the line of hats bobbing along and had heard the resounding cheers. Why then hadn't they done anything? The reply was crushing. 'Why for should ve our best vriends to kill vant'? As I have said, my sergeant's information is not always reliable. Also he is a confirmed reader of *John Bull* and of the 'Paper which Foretold the War', and doesn't love Asquith & Co.. At any rate I never heard the cheering and I very much doubt if the Germans could understand the remarks of the sanitary man who hails from one of the remotest islands in the Hebrides and speaks a language all of his own.

The 'Scrap for Y Wood', as Rule termed it, was part of the attack made on Bellewaarde Ridge – just north of the Menin Road, near Hooge – by Major-General Haldane's 3rd Division. General Haldane was later to write to the commanding officer of the 4th Gordons that he recalled the steady and soldier-like bearing of the Battalion during the attack. The 4th Gordons were attached to the 3rd Division in Belgium from the time they joined it at La Clytte on 27 February 1915, and they did not rejoin the 51st Highland Division until early in 1916. James Anderson wrote home to describe the events of a day he had been fortunate to survive, but the censor refused to pass his original letter.

My Dear Sister,

I received your letter of congrats this morning for which thanks. I described the whole days work in that letter to George which I got handed me back by the Censor. The appreciation was for voluntarily carrying messages back to the CO during the height of the German bombardment. Had some narrow escapes, but an inch is as good as a mile. So long as they don't touch you it doesn't matter. The Captain recommended me for the DCM, that is between you and myself, for I certainly did not deserve such a decoration. Enough of this – I might give you details when I come home. Well we're back in the trenches again – perfect palaces this time and very, very quiet.

How's everybody at home and where has the Sublime landed this time? – and how is Willie liking his job? I thought he was owe me a letter, but I'm beginning to think otherwise – seems that there is no signs of one. I'll have to call a halt and make some tea for my chums who will soon be back from their poaching expeditions. We're having good sport.

Goodbye and good luck,
With best wishes
from Jimmie

St Eloi and Whizzbang Wood

Almost exactly one year after their happy camp at Tain in July of 1914 U Company found itself back in the line again in the St Eloi sector, some two and a half miles south of Hooge, in what had become known as Whizzbang Wood. They were by now sadly reduced in numbers by their casualties at Hooge in June, and neither new drafts nor sufficient of their returning wounded had yet reached them to make up their strength. On 10 June Sandy Rule had confided to his diary that Pratt, by then a 2nd Lieutenant, 'had tried to put the wind up us' by telling them that all Territorial battalions below a strength of 400 were going home to recruit. By 19 June the 'fighting strength' of the 4th Gordons was given in the Battalion war diary as 18 officers and 470 other ranks and Lieut-Colonel Ogilvie went home a few days later to launch a recruiting drive. Sergeant James Fraser noted in his diary that at his last Battalion parade on 21 June 'Col Ogilvie had tears in his eyes as he looked at his Battalion, now about half strength'.

In Whizzbang Wood the Battalion found themselves facing the Saxons – it was the Saxons who had been involved in the Christmas Truce – and their appetite for war did not seem to have developed greatly in the interim. On the German parapet a sign in English proclaimed boldly: 'If you don't fire, we won't'. U Company was under orders to disturb the Saxons as much as possible as the Germans had recently used flame throwers in the Ypres Salient and their peaceful sentiments were not reciprocated. After a week the Battalion was withdrawn and found itself billeted at the White Chateau which belonged to the Hennessy Cognac family. There in the grounds they found a miniature golf course and fittingly managed to play off two golf tournaments on a handicap basis. At the outbreak of war, one of U Company's members, Alexander Cooper Jnr of the Deeside and Aberdeen Victoria Golf Clubs, was the captain-elect of the University golf team, and had been runner-up to George Thomson in the final of the Northern Amateur Championship at Lossiemouth in

1913. Cooper's father, Alexander Cooper Snr, had also been the runner-up in the Northern Amateur Championship at Lossiemouth to Dr L W Macpherson in 1898 when Macpherson won it for the third time. Another member of the 4th Gordons who took part in these golf competitions was Private George Smith who was the professional at the Deeside Golf Club before joining the Battalion. George Smith was to suffer a severe head wound at the battle of Hooge in September and was left deaf in one ear for the remainder of his life. In spite of this disability, and after being invalided out of the Gordons with a second wound, he was appointed in 1917 to the post of professional at the Moray Golf Club which he graced with his presence for 33 years.

Colonel George Cruden

The members of U Company continued to receive *Alma Mater* with their mail and must have been amused to read therein of Colonel George Cruden's exploits. George Cruden was an Aberdeen advocate who had been in command of the 1st Volunteer Battalion of the Gordon Highlanders for four years from 1900-04. He had then retired with the rank of Lieut-Colonel after 37 years service and was subsequently made an honorary Colonel of the Battalion. Frustrated in his attempts to rejoin the army at the outbreak of war, by August 1915 he had managed to enlist as a private soldier in the Royal Army Veterinary Corps. In the following year, at the age of 66, he was commissioned into the Durham Light Infantry Labour Corps and, with the rank of Captain, served in France from July 1917 to April 1918.

Colonel George Cruden

Private James 'Gamin' Anderson

About this time 'Gamin' Anderson wrote another letter to his sister describing his experiences. Anderson's original nickname as a schoolboy at Fordyce Academy had been 'Gammon', which had its origins in the smoke from the briar pipe which was his constant companion. When he arrived at university his more sophisticated student companions soon changed it to 'Gamin'.

> *16 Platoon, D Company*
> *4th Batt. Gordon Highs.*
> *BEF, France*

My Dear Sister,

I received your letter, also the parcel yesterday morning, and was delighted with the contents. The jam got a quick dispatch lasting little more than one meal, but the loaf is still holding out marvellously well. I suppose it was George who sent the pipe and cigarette lighter. Both would have been very acceptable before we went up for that long spell in the trenches but there were so many equipments lying about that we wanted for nothing - pipes, razors, shaving materials, tobacco pouches, cigarette lighters, shirts, socks etc., etc.. One chap got a splendid Waterman fountain pen, and still you don't believe we're having a picnic. Wouldn't you like to go on such expeditions - undoing packs and haversacks, and pick up whatever would be of use to you; I have often discarded my own rifle and picked up a better - 'tis all in the game.

Well, Nellie, I've been on most jobs out here. First a rifle, then rifle and stretcher-bearer and now I'm a sniper. You'll know what that means. It's the same as sitting in the den watching for rabbits. Nothing could suit me better than this, only I hope to get more fun than we did at some of our poaching expeditions. Wouldn't George [his brother-in-law] like to have a telescopic rifle? I can see him green with envy.

Well, Nellie, we're still having a high old time here out of the trenches, and still the [leave] drafts keep on going and coming. When my turn is due I cannot say, but it will take months to let us all home - let's hope I won't be the last - I don't usually have bad luck. Well, there's one thing I would like you to send out and that is a couple of pairs of socks. Meantime, good-bye and good luck. Hope all are well at home. Convey my thanks to Georgie just now, I'll write him later, and tell Robert [Robert Bruce, his three year-old nephew] I'll send him a German if he likes. How would a scalp please him? eh. I'm too horrible now. Ta ta.

> Your loving brother,
> Jimmie

By the end of August 1915 U Company had lost many of its original members. More than 20 of those who had gone to hospital wounded, and had recovered, had been commissioned as officers in other Highland regiments. The Seaforths, who had lost so many officers at the disastrous battle of Neuve Chapelle in March, claimed the largest number, but some had been commissioned into other battalions of the Gordons. The popular Company Sergeant-Major from Dyce, George (Dod) Low, MA, who had joined U Company as an 18 year-old arts student in 1910, was commissioned in August and was happy to rejoin his beloved Company as a 2nd Lieutenant. With the return of some of their wounded members - some of whom had been wounded more than once - U Company remained cheerful and confident that they could do anything that might be asked of them, and now they began preparations for what was to be their biggest test.

CHAPTER SIX

The Final Curtain

THE main battle fought by British troops under the command of Sir John French at Loos on 25 September 1915 was accompanied by a number of other smaller but simultaneous actions at various points on the British front which were described as 'containing' or 'subsidiary' battles. The 4th Gordons trained at Ouderdom for their battle at Hooge, some 20 miles to the north of the main battle, and this attack was meant to appear much more important than a containing action. The members of U Company enjoyed their preparation in excellent weather. Food was plentiful, and with the open-air exercise and a good rest at night they were soon fit and, as Alexander Rule put it, feeling in excellent form. He went on to describe their training ground.

> Early in September we left Dickebusch and camped near the tiny village of Ouderdom, where we remained until our return to the trenches some ten days afterwards. Here flies bred in myriads under ideal conditions. In addition to the normal civilian population, refugee families were huddled together in barns converted into makeshift dwellings, and sanitary arrangements were completely non-existent. A severe outbreak of dysentery was inevitable. Mosquitoes abounded, for there were many ditches full of stagnant water, filmed over with unwholesome green scum. Our camp site itself was an ideal one surrounded by pleasant fields where scarlet poppies and blue cornflowers bloomed with the changing season. If we chanced to be up with the lark, we saw the simple peasantry at their morning orisons, kneeling before flamboyant altars and images in little wayside shrines. Evenings were mild and there was twilight long after parades had finished. We lay around outside our bivouacs then, yarning and singing, until the bugles sounded Lights Out and another army day had ended. Life was never more pleasant; even the beer in Ouderdom's two modest *estaminets* seemed to us to taste all the better because it was served by bright-eyed mademoiselles.

In his diary entry for Monday 6 September 1915, Rule described the way the student soldiers prepared for the forthcoming battle. After noting that the officers promotions included Down and Falconer as captains and A R Henderson, 'Mons' and J D Pratt as lieutenants, he goes on to describe how they practised the plan for the attack. It was 'great fun and a good few of them fell into a ditch in the excitement of the "charge" – we could scarcely take the [German] third line for laughing!' He wrote home at this time about another preparation for the forthcoming battle.

> Dear Jeannie,
>
> I am afraid I am letting my correspondence get the better of me but I am going to scrawl a short note just now. A good many of the Company took Communion yesterday for the first time. We had a sort of preparatory service on Saturday night at

the Chaplain's tent. We made a half circle round the door and the Chaplain made a few remarks about the solemnity of Communion and how it was instituted. It was a very nice service indeed. At the close the Chaplain took down all our names and addresses also church and minister.

Yesterday (Sunday) we had the usual service in the forenoon then Communion Service at 6 p.m. at the door of the Chaplain's tent. The service was attended by Major Lyon, Commanding Officer, Capt. Hopkinson whom father knows, and two lieuts.. A strange lull seemed to occur in the dull sound of the guns and the evening itself was an ideal summer evening. The long slanting rays of the sinking sun showed up the golden harvest of man as it lay stooked in the fields around. Over the firing line the clouds were bathed in golden light and in the distance could be seen small mounds crowned with windmills....

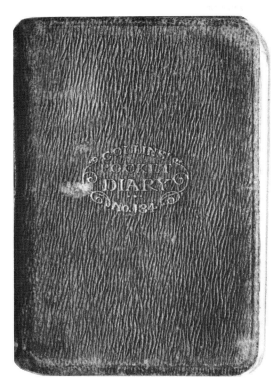

Alexander Rule's diary

Rule's letter to his sister - censored by Walter Inkster

Dysentery

The problem of dysentery referred to by Rule was not uncommon in France and Belgium in 1915. John Knowles, in a letter to his friend John McConachie in March of 1915, stated that although the food was quite good and nourishing, yet almost everyone was suffering from a bowel complaint. This was not a peculiar disease of the French. Both in Britain and on the continent in these early days of the war, the horse was the chief method of transport and as a result there was a large amount of horse manure lying about. This was an ideal source for flies spreading infection and gave rise to the old medical student's alliterative mnemonic that the principal cause of dysentery was the 'filthy feet of faecal feeding flies'. Even as late as the 1920s the epidemics of so-called 'summer diarrhoea' in Britain were attended by a considerable mortality rate in babies, but these outbreaks ceased as the horse was replaced by the motor car.

The Jocks' Society

Some of the livelier members of U Company, 15 in all, had formed themselves into 'The Jocks' Society' – also known as 'The Society of Good Johns' – and their last meeting took place on Wednesday 22 September 1915. It was subsequently described in the February 1917 number of *Alma Mater* by Robert Stewart. Stewart had become an enthusiastic member of U Company as a first year arts student in 1910 and was fortunate to survive the coming battle and resume his studies. He graduated MA with honours in mathematics in 1916 and became a teacher at Robert Gordon's College after the war.

"The Only Girl in the World"

Or the only one within five miles of the trenches!

It is with mixed feelings that we recall the last meeting of the Jocks' Society – a genuine University gathering – for we were wont to assemble in rest billets, after our day's work was done, and forget Belgium and its mud, in sweet retrospection.

The memorable day, September 22nd 1915, with all its bustle and preparation passed. Evening fell, and the distant guns beat a muffled tattoo, as, our day's drill over, we left our humble bivouacs and sought the unpretentious precincts of a neighbouring farmhouse, the rendez-vous of the Jocks' Society. This, though we refused to believe it, was to be our last meeting, for on the morrow we were to be moving up to the trenches, preparatory to the September push in the Hooge Salient.

But the spirit of U Company rose above sinister premonitions for the future, and laughter and song ran around the rough deal table of the farm kitchen.

It had been the custom of University men in the Battalion to meet here, and over a frugal dish of potatoes and sauce (*erypels* – in the patois of the district) to discuss subjects of common interest, and Alma Mater figured largely in the conversation. Those of us who were privileged to attend will recall the scene – Sergeant Crichton in the presidential chair maintained order with zest in debates. The speeches of such as Privates Mason and Surtees were received with keen relish, and appreciated as literary delicacies by their hearers, while Peterkin's caustic humour, usually directed against some members of the Society, and Sunny's [McLellan] subtlety added greatly to the enjoyment of the evening.

Supper over, we gathered round the heart of the open fireplace and the past occupied our thoughts. Marischal College, with all its joys and associations, was discussed, and many a wish expressed that soon, notebook in hand, we would again cross the quadrangle. No mention of the morrow was made.

Soon we heard the first post blown and before departing, the strains of *Gaudeamus* – sung with great fervour – echoed far and wide.

The Battle at Hooge

The Brigade the 4th Gordons were attached to was inspected and addressed by Field Marshal Lord Kitchener on 22 September, and he left the Gordons in no doubt that the attack at Hooge was in the nature of a sacrifice to help the main offensive. Kitchener, who was accompanied by Generals Allenby and Haldane, congratulated them on the honour and responsibility which had fallen on them as a Territorial unit and, in a curious phrase, wished them as much luck as they could expect. Rule recalled that no attempt had been made to conceal their preparations from the enemy, so much so that the Germans had placards on their barbed wire reading: 'Why not attack today, Jocks? Why wait for the 25th'?

The Germans expected a big battle in the Ypres Salient and for more than a month had been assembling a large force of men and guns. They were not disappointed, and on Saturday 25 September 1915 the expected attack took place. It extended from the British assembly position in the trenches at Sanctuary Wood to north of the Menin Road, and the 4th Gordons, commanded by Lieut-Colonel Alexander Lyon, advanced in the centre with the 1st Gordons on their left and the 2nd Royal Scots on their right. The objective was known as 'Stirling Castle', about 1200 yards in depth. After an artillery bombardment of the German lines and the exploding of three mines, at ten past four in the morning, in pouring rain, the three kilted battalions went up their ladders, out of the trenches and over the top into the semi-darkness of No Man's Land. This was indeed Dante's Inferno with bursting shells and bombs and a hail of bullets from rifles and machine guns – and then they encountered the uncut enemy wire. U Company were fortunate in that the belts of wire ahead of them had been cut in one or two places, and the use of wire cutters, in a slightly protected hollow in the ground which concealed them, enabled them to get through to and take the lightly-held German front line. As they lay on the German parapet waiting for their guns to lift from their next objective, they watched the headlong charge by the 1st Gordons on their left into a deadly rifle and machine-gun fire, and into a wide belt of completely uncut wire. The few surviving men of the 1st ran along the front of the wire until they came to the 4th Gordons' front and carried on the attack with them.

U Company and the 4th Gordons carried their advance over three lines of enemy trenches, but by then many had been killed in fierce hand-to-hand fighting and only a handful of men were unwounded. The Brigade diary for the 25th records that at 5.50 am the 4th Gordons reported that they had taken the German third line. Casualties were very heavy, particularly among officers. At 8 am a report was received that they held Fort 13, their objective, and that they had captured a field gun, but that the Germans were bombarding them heavily.

The survivors were forced to withdraw to the old German first line as enemy bombing parties worked in from their flanks and steadily reduced the area they were holding. U Company's own miserable stock of bombs soon gave out and the emery paper used as a primitive method of igniting the fuse of the bomb became wet and useless in the rain. The Germans counter-attacked fiercely and the remnants of the three Scottish battalions who had attacked with great courage and discipline, fell back to the positions they had started from. The combined casualty list of the 1st and 4th Gordons was thirty-two officers and six hundred and thirty-five other ranks killed and wounded. No ground had been gained but the High Command deemed the battle a success. The enemy had been prevented from sending reinforcements to Loos.

Writing in 1958, long after the second war, the eminent military historian Sir Cyril Falls took a different view. In *The Life of a Regiment - The Gordon Highlanders in the First World War* - he had this to say.

> Between eleven a.m. and noon the Germans [counter] attacked both across the open and along the trenches. After a fierce struggle the 4th Gordons and such of the 1st as had got in [to the German trenches] were driven out. That was the general pattern of the action in which no success was gained at any point. The troops could not have done more. The battalions of the Gordons suffered heavy loss, approximately the same; but the 1st had by far the higher proportion of wounded, shot down outside the wire, and the 4th of missing, cut off in the blocked trenches. In the whole operation just short of two hundred [German] prisoners had been captured, but the German losses must have been light by comparison with the British. As a diversion the operations had been of no avail because the Germans had been able to contain the attack with local reserves which would in no case have been moved down to the main battlefield south of the La Bassée canal.

The conclusions Falls draws make interesting reading today and show something of the courage and determination of the young men who fought with the Gordons.

> It may therefore not be surprising that despite the sharp disappointment and the heavy loss, the majority of the surviving officers and men gained, rather than lost, confidence. They felt that such a chapter of accidents and errors could not recur, and that they themselves had proved better men than even in their proudest moments they had claimed to be. In the last respect they were right, but accident and error are an eternal feature of war which only those who have never fought will mock.

The battle was over for the Gordons at Hooge, but further south at Loos the 21st and 24th divisions went into action on the second day. At eleven o'clock in broad daylight they went over the top into a No Man's Land where there was no cover and which was strewn with the bodies of the Highlanders (some of the five battalions of Gordons amongst them) and the English regiments who had attacked on the previous day. The 12 British battalions thrown into the second day's fighting sustained over 8000 casualties while the Germans had none. It is said that the German machine gunners finally stopped firing to allow the wounded survivors to get back to their own lines. This episode went down in German military history as the *Leichenfeld von Loos* - the 'corpsefield of Loos'. After the war the British official historian Brigadier Sir James Edmonds wrote of Loos that 'it brought nothing but misfortune and disappointment, for which mismanagement was partly responsible'.

When the news of the disaster reached London very strong feelings began to surface over what was seen as a massacre. Lord Haldane was sent out to France to get the facts from General Haig and the upshot was that the 63 year-old Sir John French was relieved of his command two months later on 19 December 1915 and Sir Douglas Haig was appointed Commander-in-Chief of all the forces of the Empire from 1 January 1916. The Loos disaster - in which the British had 50,000 casualties against the Germans' 20,000 - also saw the end of the last Liberal Government in Britain.

Asquith had already formed a coalition government with the aid of the Conservative and Labour parties, with Lloyd George – who had publicly expressed the opinion that 'war was too serious a matter to be left to the Generals' – as the Minister for Munitions. On 6 December 1916, Lloyd George became Prime Minister.

The British press was not intrusive in those days and the sacking of Sir John French was reported in an appropriate manner. French himself told Winston Churchill that pressures had been applied to him to relinquish his command without a row. Newspapers large and small carried the War Office's announcement that; – 'General Sir Douglas Haig has been appointed to succeed Sir John French, the latter having felt the sixteen months of severe and incessant strain and has now, at his own instance, relinquished his command. The Field Marshal has been raised to the Peerage as a Viscount and has accepted the post of Commander-in-Chief of the troops stationed in the United Kingdom'. The editorial writers were no less graceful, with *The Times* commenting that; – 'On the shoulders of Sir Douglas Haig there has now been placed a great burden, but he has a fine record in France, and those who may give an opinion on the subject highly eulogise the successor of even so great a commander as General French'.

Sir John French

Casualties at Hooge

The 4th Battalion of the Gordons suffered severe casualties at Hooge. Alexander Rule was one of the wounded in U Company and he recalled that when he asked his rescuers about the rest of the Company he was told that they were all either killed, wounded or missing. The Battalion Diary (in the HQ of the Regiment in Aberdeen) of the 4th Gordons for 25 September 1915 sets out the cost in print. The fighting strength before the battle was 27 officers and 630 other ranks.

Casualties as far as at present known

NCOs & Men	A Company	B Company	C Company	D(U) Company	Totals
Killed	3	10	6	4	23
Died of wounds	1	-	-	-	1
Wounded	23	43	36	46	148
Wounded & Missing	-	-	4	2	6
Missing	5	19	65	52	141
Totals	**32**	**72**	**111**	**104**	**319**

Of the officers, seven were missing, seven were wounded and one was known to have been killed. The list of casualties was remarkably accurate and the final figures were substantially unchanged. As so often happened in the Great War the missing in D Company were all subsequently reported killed except for Private Robert Wilson, an arts student, who was taken prisoner by the Germans. Captain Hopkinson, the company commander, and both platoon commanders, 2nd Lieutenant Walter Inkster MA, BSc, and 2nd Lieutenant W J C Sangster, MA, were all later confirmed as killed in action.

The order of battle on 25 September had been for two platoons of B Company to take the German first line and for C and D Companies acting together to take the second and third lines. The Roll Call that evening was - B Company 17 men: C Company 18 men: D Company 32 men. Two weeks later *Alma Mater* carried a heavily censored report in a short 'Letter from the Front' which ended - 'The double Company 'D' is the amalgamation of the Aberdeen University and Gordon's College and Grammar School Companies'.

On Monday 27 September, two days after the battle at Hooge, the Commander of the 3rd Division, Major-General J A L Haldane, himself an old Gordon Highlander, came and addressed the Battalion. He explained the situation and the necessity of 'containing' attacks and complimented the 4th Gordons very strongly in the way they had attacked. The Battalion diary for 2 October 1915 stated baldly - 'Still in the trenches. All ranks feeling the strain - not having recovered properly from the attack. Men a bit grumpy. Sergeant Crichton wounded. Draft of nine re-joined men and fifteen new men arrived'.

Censorship of news

It is almost impossible today to comprehend the severity of the censorship which prevented any accurate news of what had happened on the battlefield ever reaching the newspapers and the general public. War correspondents were few and were confined to the area of General Headquarters which was far removed from the front, and what little news they were allowed to send home was heavily censored. There was no question of a newspaper correspondent simply lifting a telephone and telling his editor what he knew. This can be the only explanation for the news carried in the *Aberdeen Daily Journal* on Monday 27 September, two days after the disaster for the Gordons. The editorial was headed 'Good News From The West' and appeared as usual after the column headed *Society and Personal*.

The news from the western theatre of war is the best that has reached us for many months. Indeed, apart from the successful resistance opposed to the great German efforts to capture Calais, there has been no success equal in magnitude and importance to those which the British and French forces, operating at widely separated parts of the long front, have achieved during the weekend. In the communiqué published in Berlin on Friday it was asserted that an attack by British and coloured troops in the neighbourhood of La Bassée broke down under the fire of the German artillery. That report was premature and, as Sir John French informs us, likewise false. But the attack has now been delivered and it has by no means broken down. On the contrary it is the German defence, believed by the enemy to be impregnable, which has collapsed. Along a front of five miles their trenches to the south of the La Bassée canal are now in the occupation of the British troops to a depth which at several points approaches 4000 yards. This is a greater feat than was accomplished by our troops in March at Neuve Chapelle when ground over two miles in length by some 1200 yards in breadth was captured. It is to be feared that our casualties will prove heavy, but provided that the infantry attack was preceded by a devastating bombardment with high explosive shells which swept away all obstacles to the advance, it will probably be found that our losses are proportionately fewer than those we suffered at Neuve Chapelle.

On the same date as the above appeared, *The Times* carried an editorial headed 'The German Line Pierced in the West' which contained the following paragraph.

We regret that a series of operations in which the British Army has played so prominent and successful a part should be so scantily recorded. We have necessarily laid principal stress upon the French advance in Champagne, because it appears to be the chief feature of the new offensive. Yet the British Army has apparently also made the most considerable advance won by British arms since our Expeditionary Force shared in the glory of the battle of the Marne. Could the story of Saturday's action have been told in some fullness, under due restrictions, it would have carried a message of joy to countless British homes. Presumably we shall learn the details in driblets, from Dutch or American sources, to which the Press of this country is now compelled to turn for information which is often of doubtful validity. The nation needs cheering, and the present occasion seems to have afforded a suitable opportunity.

The short-lived euphoria was added to by Colonel F Maude, the 'well-known military expert', in a lecture at New Brighton on the situation on the Western Front, which was reported in the *Aberdeen Daily Journal* on 29 September. He declared that there was now every possibility that the Allies would be able to drive the Germans steadily back on the western frontier. With reasonable luck they should have them up against the Rhine within two months, he contended. The Allies had not attempted to do everything at one blow. They had consolidated every step won, and should be able to go on repeating the performance until the end came. The Allies had evidently flattened out the enemy, silenced his guns, and broken his power of resistance. He thought that it was probable that the end of the war would come as a great surprise.

Perhaps the most revealing comment on censorship during the Great War was made by Lloyd George. The great Liberal journalist C P Scott was the editor of the *Manchester Guardian* from 1872-1929 and his paper had taken a resolute anti-war stance in 1914. However, when Lloyd George became Prime Minister in December 1916 he found that – in the main – he could rely on the newspaper for support, and his friendship with his old ally C P Scott was a close one. In *Tempestuous Journey*, published in 1954, Frank Owen described how the journalist called on the tired and over-worked Prime Minister in December 1917, at the end of the year of the Battle of Passchendaele, and found him almost in despair.

'I warn you', said Lloyd George, 'I am in a very pacifist temper. I listened last night at a dinner given to Philip Gibbs [the war correspondent] on his return from the Front, to the most impressive and moving description from him of what the war in the West really means, that I have heard. Even an audience of hardened politicians and journalists was strongly affected. If people really new, the war would be stopped tomorrow, but of course they don't know – and can't know. The [war] Correspondents don't write, and the Censorship wouldn't pass the truth. The thing is horrible, and beyond human nature to bear, and I feel I can't go on any longer with the bloody business: I would rather resign.

Return to Aberdeen

Suddenly, in October 1915, the 'Foot Companions' of U Company had ceased to exist and the few men who remained fit were incorporated in the fresh drafts from home to form a new D Company. After the battle, Captain Down was describing U Company when he wrote to 'his only Phyllis' on September 27: – 'I saw six men and a juvenile NCO coming along the road. As they passed I hailed the leader. "Why aren't you marching home with your platoon?" "Platoon, Sir", he answered, "This is D Company".'

The majority of the unwounded survivors of U Company soldiered on as officers with much battle experience, and a further 16 of them lost their lives - very few escaped the war unwounded. The wounded and the unfit went before medical boards and gradually drifted back to their studies - although a number of them spent a long time in hospital. As they walked to their classes at King's or Marischal College in the soft spring breezes of the following year, perhaps they whistled a bar or two of *Gaudeamus* and thought of their many friends who had failed to answer *adsum* at the final Roll-Call. Maybe they felt that if there was a Valhalla, the members of U Company would be there - clad in their scarlet tunics, kilts and white spats - and seated far above the salt.

A Memorial Volume for the Fallen

PRESENTED

BY

THE UNIVERSITY OF ABERDEEN

in memory of

John Forbes Knowles

UNIVERSITY OF ABERDEEN

ROLL OF SERVICE

IN THE GREAT WAR

1914-1919

EDITED BY

MABEL DESBOROUGH ALLARDYCE

ABERDEEN UNIVERSITY PRESS

M · CM · XXI

CHAPTER SEVEN

A Chaplain's Address

EVERYONE in Aberdeen in 1915 knew someone who had a son, a nephew, a brother, cousin or friend serving with the 4th Gordons and the citizens of Aberdeen were stunned by the news of what had happened to the Battalion. From the communiqués printed in their local newspaper they gleaned that the battle which had been fought at Loos had been a victory for the Allies, but they knew nothing of the 'containing' action at Hooge. Was it part of the great victory, and what exactly did a 'containing action' mean? The casualties among the Gordons were the main topic of conversation, and particularly so at the church services on the following Sunday. The many churches in the city were filled to overflowing as the ministers preached to the packed and largely uncomprehending congregations. The very large numbers of 'missing' reported in the daily casualty lists raised the hope that many of these would turn out to be prisoners of war.

The four Companies in the 4th Battalion of the Gordons had a total of 147 missing; 65 of these were in C Company and 52 in D (U) Company. The melancholy fact was that the great majority of those reported missing had been killed in the battle, although this took some time to establish. It was not until September 1916 that the War Office was able to confirm that George Low, the popular Sergeant-Major and subsequently a 2nd Lieutenant with U Company, had lost his life at Hooge. Low had refused to retire from the captured German trenches, and when last seen he was surrounded and firing his revolver at the enemy. The *Banffshire Herald* of 1 July 1916 carried a report of the annual prize-giving at Fordyce Academy where it was announced that one of their old schoolboys, Alexander Findlater, had been missing for nine months. Findlater, a previous dux of the Academy and a nephew of Piper Findlater of the Gordons who won the VC at Dargai, was later listed amongst the killed at Hooge.

George Low

It was a minister, the Reverend A M MacLean, CMG, BD, of Paisley Abbey, who, as seen below, would tell the people of Aberdeen as much as they would ever know about the events at Hooge on that fateful Saturday in September. Although small items, readily seized on, appeared in the local and national newspapers, they revealed very little to relatives and friends anxious for more news. Short extracts from letters, written by Lt-Colonel Alexander Lyon to the parents of wounded officers, which were printed in the *Aberdeen Daily Journal* were read eagerly, but there was little of consequence for those seeking comfort for almost six months until the Reverend A M MacLean - who had been at Hooge as chaplain with the 1st Gordons - delivered an emotional address to a packed congregation in the West (United Free) Parish Church in Aberdeen on the evening of Sunday 5 March 1916.

As a result of the fierce censorship in operation during the Great War, largely, it must be said, aimed at creating an illusion of victory and lauding the military leaders, the local newspapers were quite unable to inform the citizens of Aberdeen of the reasons for the huge losses in killed and wounded suffered by the Gordons in the battle at Hooge. The relatives and friends of the soldiers had no information about what had happened, apart from the snippets in the newspapers and the accounts of the wounded returning to Aberdeen. This address by a chaplain with the British Expeditionary Force who had been present and watched the battle at a distance was greeted avidly as an attempt to explain in part what had occurred to the Gordons on that dreadful September day.

J K Forbes

The effectiveness of the censorship was further illustrated with the publication in October 1916 of *Student and Sniper-Sergeant*, a memoir of J K Forbes. This book, written by his friends William Taylor MA and Peter Diack MA, and published more than a year after Forbes was killed, was reviewed in the *Banffshire Advertiser* of 19 October 1916. The review was headed 'A Hero of Loos - The story of J K', and read in part:-

When the memorable day of Loos arrived on 25th September he was no laggard in the fight. He was one of the first to leap from the trenches, and led the battalion in the charge. He made straight for a vicious machine gun which was spitting death, killed the three gunners with his own hand, and himself received a slight wound. On his way back to the dressing station this intrepid soldier was killed by bursting shrapnel, and the dauntless heart of the hero, who could sit calmly on Hill 60 reading his Greek Testament, was stilled for ever. The gallant Gordons lost many brave men that day, but none more beloved than JK.

The reviewer, writing in a very carefully edited Aberdeenshire newspaper, had no idea - even 12 months after the event - that the 4th Gordons had fought in a battle at Hooge which was more than 20 miles away from the main British battle at Loos.

STUDENT AND
SNIPER-SERGEANT

A MEMOIR OF

J. K. FORBES, M.A.

4TH BATTALION GORDON HIGHLANDERS
WHO DIED FOR HIS COUNTRY, 25 SEPTEMBER, 1915

BY

WILLIAM TAYLOR, M.A.

AND

PETER DIACK, M.A.

HODDER AND STOUGHTON
LONDON   NEW YORK   TORONTO
MCMXVI

Address by the Reverend A M MacLean CMG BD on 5 March 1916

This address was subsequently printed and published in April 1916 as a small paper-backed book, costing one shilling, after many requests from the people of Aberdeen. In his foreword to the book the writer stated that the address was delivered in the presence of many officers and men who were personally familiar with most of the incidents referred to – and went on to say that the repulse of the 8th Brigade at Hooge seemed to be due to the insuperable barrier of wire which confronted the Gordons.

With the Gordons at Ypres

I have come to Aberdeen to discharge what is to me a very sacred duty. I think that the people of this country have as yet only a dim sense of the part which their sons have played in this titanic war. Military exigencies have woven a veil of secrecy over events and episodes and personalities which will one day furnish the most thrilling pages in the long and splendid story of our race. The war correspondent has been banished from the field. Those who participate in the struggle are rightly debarred from recording their impressions for public use at the time. The official dispatches are necessarily cryptic, and do no more than indicate the enthralling human interest of the drama.

Disadvantages of Secrecy

There can be no question as to the entire wisdom of this phenomenal secrecy. But it has certain obvious disadvantages. When the men in the field have taken part in combats in which they have displayed the highest military virtues and endured the heaviest losses, and they find the Homeric struggle dismissed in some such phrase as 'In the Ypres Salient there was a containing movement', it is apt to be a little discouraging.

But that is the very least of it. The really serious element is the effect which is produced upon our unimaginative people at home. If for one single day only, the men who are working in security at home had an experience of the conditions of modern warfare there would be no strikes, no restriction of output, but an intense, resolute and sustained determination to put every ounce of strength, at no matter what personal sacrifice, into the grim task of prosecuting the war. After all the Welsh miners and the Clyde operatives are the blood-brothers of the men in the trenches. [There had been strikes]. There is no reason to doubt that they possess the same racial qualities which have made the whole Army illustrious. They are dour in sticking to their futile theories of individualism, just as their brothers are *dour* in holding on to the trenches. But they are invincibly ignorant. They are living in a fool's paradise, which the long-sheltered years have built around them, and they cannot even imagine what the storm means which is raging without, and which may at any moment overwhelm them.

The Effects of 'Frightfulness'

The Germans mercifully do not understand the character of the British people. (We are not the only people who make mistakes). They have persuaded themselves that by a calculated policy of 'frightfulness' they will bring us to our knees, and they have sent out their submarines and Zeppelins to produce a moral effect which they imagine will be decisive. From the bottom of our hearts we thank them. What! frighten the race whose virile qualities they have proved to their cost in the trenches at Ypres. Nay; they are rousing us to the realities of war, and bringing home to us the evil in whose very existence our people obstinately refused to believe. I have often thought that if the Germans had relied upon their military prowess and observed a studious chivalry in the conduct of the war they would have beaten us before we were awake and aware. But they are accelerating our education. Not only do they reap no military advantage from the policy of frightfulness, but they are rousing against them forces which will prove their undoing. When the men in the workshops know what the men in the trenches know, a spirit will be born in this nation which will go forth like a whirlwind of doom and destroy the inhuman tyranny which is dominated by the insensate lust of conquest and recognises no rights of interest but its own. Already that spirit has glorified France, and invested our Allies with a heroism which is sublime. We have not yet attained to the moral grandeur of France, but the day is near when we shall be worthy to stand beside her in defence of all that we hold dear.

A Tribute and an Appeal

My object, therefore, in speaking to you tonight is a two-fold one. I wish to lift a corner of the veil which has concealed in large measure the immortal deeds of our men, and to appeal to their countrymen at home to rise to the full height of the opportunities of these epoch-making days and prove themselves worthy of the men who have fought and died to preserve for us our ancient heritage of civilisation. And remember, I beg of you, that I do not speak for myself alone. I am the bearer of a message. I can never forget the Gordons, but I promised them within sight of the ruined towers of Ypres that I would not cease to work or plead for them, and here in Aberdeen, the home of the Gordons, I shall try – as I have tried elsewhere – to discharge my duty to the lads I love and reverence with all my heart and soul.

A Year of Service

For a twelvemonth I had the honour to serve as a chaplain with the British Expeditionary Force. My experience was, I believe, an unusually varied one, extending from the base to the front line, and in the course of it I have ministered to units of every Scottish regiment except the Scots Guards and the Scots Greys. But all the time I was brought curiously in contact with the Gordons, and I am not disposed to deny that they had a peculiar fascination for me which led me into very intimate relations with them, on which I was often playfully rallied by my brother officers. I suspect that the secret of it was that my first charge was the parish of Turriff in Aberdeenshire, and my first chaplaincy was the post which your minister [the Reverend J Esslemont Adams, DSO, MC] is holding now with the 6th Gordons, and you know there is no love like the first love. Besides, I was old enough to meet in the ranks many lads I had baptised, and therefore you will perhaps not wonder at the attraction which the tartan with the yellow stripe had for me.

The Reinforcement Camp

All last winter and spring I acted as chaplain to the Scottish troops in the chief Reinforcement Camp in France. Right opposite my tent were the lines of the Gordons. I preached to them on Sundays. I saw them daily in their tents. With the generous help of hosts of well-wishers in all parts of Scotland, I saved hundreds of them from the penalties of a defective kit! And none of them left for the front without the padre's blessing. I went to every train in which Scottish troops were going up the line, entered each compartment, and personally handed to every man a gift, which was to him the symbol of the loving interest of the homeland, addressed the men briefly, urging them to bear in mind the high interests committed to their trust, and shook hands with every one of them, praying that God might give them stout hearts and strong arms. It was hard work, and fruitful in many surprising ways, and I wish I could tell you the story in detail, for it was full of human interest; but though I had to deal with many thousands of Scottish troops, my business here tonight is to speak of the Gordons; and therefore I will confine myself to a single incident which will perhaps give you an illuminating glimpse of the variety and utility of the padre's work.

I had not been long in that great camp when I became conscious of a curious omission. There we were in the midst of the most nerve-wracking war that the world has ever seen, and though the power of martial music to sustain the human spirit has been recognised since the beginning of time, not a note of music was heard in the camp or on the march - neither band nor pipes nor bugle nor drum. Our chiefs were too absorbed in their gigantic efforts to provide the bare necessities of warfare to think of luxuries like these. I set to work to remedy the defect, and through the generosity of the Scottish Flag Day Committee, procured several sets of bagpipes which were distributed so as to secure that no Scottish unit should go up the line without the inspiring strains of their native music to cheer them on their way.

The Ypres Salient

It was a beautiful country in those shining summer days, and on the rare occasions when the guns were silent, it was difficult to believe in the reality of war. It seemed like a dreadful nightmare in the glowing light of noon. But the gaunt towers of Ypres rose out of billowy masses of wood, wearing not the imploring beauty of decay but an even more pathetic and alluring aspect of recent agony. The neighbouring villages of Vlamertinghe and Dickebusch and Kruisstraat, between which we shifted from camp to camp, were being pounded systematically by what Tommy calls 'heavy stuff'. The moment you enter the crumbling streets, rent and shattered, and reeking with the pungent smell of mortar, the illusion of the country disappeared and you were face to face with the reality of the cruel wrath of man. You cannot get away from the guns near Ypres. I appreciated the snarl in a friend's letter when he wrote a few weeks ago - 'Conscientious objectors forsooth! Half an hour in the beastly Salient would give them something to object to'.

Church Parade

The services on Sunday were held in the open fields or in a wood, for in the Ypres Salient we were never for one moment beyond the range of the guns and hostile aeroplanes were constantly spying for a mark. I remember one Sunday a very strange and impressive incident at the Gordon service. We happened to be singing the very words - 'Yea, though I walk in death's dark vale, Yet will I fear none ill', when I heard the whistle of a shell behind me. It grew louder and louder, rushing like a railway train overhead, and burst with a crashing roar half a mile away near where the 4th Gordons were bivouacked. I remember thinking at the moment that the most gifted organist could not have achieved with all the resources of his art such a solemnising accompaniment as it provided for the words we were singing. But not a man in the ranks before me moved a muscle, and I hope the padre kept his countenance too.

You will perhaps, not be surprised when I tell you that in the midst of the experiences which the men had daily to undergo, the services were unlike any I have known. When a shell may obliterate you and your congregation it makes for reality. The preacher must speak the essential message, and the men listen with their whole heart and soul, for they know - they know that the things which are seen are temporal and they hope that the things which are unseen are eternal. What did I say to them? Why, think a moment. These were fine lads - your sons and brothers - in the springtime of their life, daily face to face with suffering and death, not seeking the bubble reputation at the cannon's mouth, but hating and loathing the hideous cruelties of war, yet impelled by a stern sense of duty to give up life and youth and love and fair dreams - for you, for their country, for the high cause of human freedom, for the redemption of mankind from the insatiable lust of evil. The substitutes of humanity - like Christ himself - they were the saviours of the world - and from the Master Spirit alone, and kneeling before His cross, would they learn the secret which makes men laugh at death and follow duty like a shining star. Yes, the Cross of Christ is the only message which will do for the lads at the front. And they are taking it all in. I tell you they are taking it all in.

The Battle of 25th September

The great event during my period of service with the Gordons was the battle of the 25 September – wrongly called the Battle of Loos, for it was an attack ranging from Switzerland to the sea. The real point of the British attack was at Loos, and of the French in Champagne. Our share in it was summarised in the dispatches in the words 'In the Ypres Salient there was a containing movement' – but oh! the tragedy and the splendour that are hidden under that prosaic official phrase. I have already trespassed greatly upon your patience, but will you bear with me while I try to give you a fleeting glimpse of its epic grandeur?

The Eve of Battle

The preparations for the attack were thorough and prolonged, and little attempt at concealment was made. I suppose it was part of the plan to give the impression that the crowning stroke would be delivered at Ypres. Lord Kitchener himself came out and inspected the Royal Scots and the 1st and 4th Gordons. He told them that 'Scotland expected that their work would be thoroughly well done'. There was a listening padre on parade who made the mental comment that there would be no doubt about that. The Sunday before we had a very solemn communion; for many it was their last communion on earth. On the night before the attack I had special services with both the Royals and the Gordons, and I know not what the spirit of Cromwell's Ironsides was, but it could not have been more deep and devout and heroic than theirs. Ah! Scotland may well be proud of her sons.

That night I sat for long in my tent, and one by one the officers and men came in with letters and keepsakes which I enclosed in envelopes inscribed with the givers' names and the names of those to whom they were to be sent if need be. Little was said, but the tight hand-grip showed all. That night too, I heard the most moving speech I ever listened to. It was the occasion that made it. Sitting on his horse in the midst of his glorious men, Colonel Percy Brown of the [1st] Gordons told them what they had to do in brief, stern words, and bade them 'remember the name of the regiment'. Like a greyhound straining at the leash, they answered him with ringing cheers, and so they went into battle carrying their heads high and with the steel glint in their eyes.

A Sublime Spectacle

On the night of the attack, the four Scots padres went to a height overlooking and close by the lines. We saw the red surge of war breaking on the trenches from Hooge to La Bassée, and the roar of the guns was like the thunder of the Hebridean seas. As I lay on the ground with my eyes glued to my field-glasses, straining to pierce the darkness which gathered over Hooge, I saw the stabbing flashes of our guns suddenly extinguished and huge mushrooms of red flame leaping to the sky along the German lines where our mines were sprung; and I prayed that God might be with my boys and show His mercy to those passing into His presence. Along the lines of the trenches a continuous band of lurid fire showed the intensity of the German artillery resistance; it seemed as if no living thing could cross that unbroken zone of death. With the coming of the misty dawn which made farther observation fruitless, we returned to the posts which we were instructed to hold in battle. Mr Scott's [Thomas Scott of Laurencekirk, chaplain to the 4th Gordons] and mine were at the advanced dressing station through which most of the wounded of our brigade would pass on their way to the casualty clearing station behind. There we should learn what the darkness had hidden from our eyes. We had not long to wait. Bad news travels fast. The attack had failed, and it had failed because the 1st Gordons and the English regiment on their left could not reach the objective assigned to them – this seemed to be due to the insuperable barrier of wire which confronted them. Oh! the anguish of these hours of waiting till we should learn exactly what had happened. But bit by bit the story unfolded itself – told to us in snatches by many broken men – and if it was a tragedy, thank God! it was a tragedy aflame with glory.

The Charge

When the guns ceased and the whistles sounded the charge, the long line of Scots leaped the parapet as one man. If the ghosts of the old Royals who fought over these very fields under Marlborough were looking down on their successors that day they must have been well content. Like a living torrent Colonel Duncan and his men [the 2nd Royal Scots] rushed upon the German trenches and held them. On their left flank the 4th Gordons kept pace with Scotland's premier regiment and did not yield them a single point of honour. Colonel Lyon and the sons of Aberdeen showed that day, as the 4th Camerons had done at Neuve Chapelle, that there is nothing to choose between regulars and Territorials. On the left flank of the 4th, the 1st Gordons hurled themselves impetuously forward, and one company and part of another reached their objective abreast of the Territorials and the Royal Scots. But there the tragedy began. For some reason or other the maze of barbed wire in front of the remaining company and a half of the Gordons and the English regiment on their left had escaped the pulverising artillery fire and was intact. The Englishmen reached the wire and finding it insuperable wisely retired to their trenches. Not so the Gordons. On to the wire they surged, tried to get over it, to get under it, to get through it, and there on the wire they died, but they would not go back. Captain Menteith was shot in the arm as he cleared the parapet. He bound up the wound and went on. For the third time he went out, reached the wire, and there too, he died.

Unavailing Valour

So the attack had failed, and the part of the line which had succeeded was 'in the air'. On the extreme left a solitary 1st Gordon was seen with his leg blown off at the knee propping up against the trench and coolly throwing bombs over the traverse to check the German onrush, till he pitched forward on his face and died. Two sergeants who saw the incident knew him by sight but could not recall his name – so quickly do men pass through the battalions in these days of stress. And so he remains a nameless hero, but typical of all. Slowly and sullenly the 4th Gordons retired. The Royal Scots were the last to leave. Yet it had to be. The attack had failed. But the staff, it seems, were more than satisfied. This was only 'a containing movement'. The real push was far down the line at Loos. Yet such had been the concentrated fury of the Scots' attack that the Germans in alarm had been compelled to hurry up a division of the Prussian Guards, and so the movement had surpassed the expectation of the controlling mind. But oh! the cruel cost of it all, and the agony of those days when we only knew what was happening upon our own particular segment of the battle-line.

At the Dressing Station

All that day I was engaged in burying the dead. Through the following night the wounded came streaming in faster than they could be evacuated. Their condition was pitiable, for a cold, clammy rain had fallen persistently all day. Yet I never heard a murmur. Yes; I heard one. A young Aberdeen student, with a finely chiselled face, lay on the table while the surgeon tried to give him unavailing relief, and as I held his hand he moaned out his sorrow over the failure of his battalion to hold the trenches they had won. I saw a Scot lying on the ground, plastered from head to foot in mud as with a trowel. I thought I recognised the yellow stripe in the tartan, and stepping gently over an unconscious form between, I touched him and said, 'Are you a 1st Gordon, my lad'? His arm was crushed, his leg was twisted, but the white of his eye gleamed through the mud that caked his face as he answered with an unmistakable grin, "A wis this mornin', and 'a think a'm a half yin yet'. And then in a moment he knew me, and reaching out his only hand he gripped me tight and said, 'Oh! minister, it's you. Ye might write to my wife and dinna frighten her. A'll be a' richt yet'. What a superb spirit! A jest for his own misery and the tenderest consideration for those at home. Such are the men who are bearing all for you on these grim fields of Flanders.

104

Still the 'Gay Gordons'.

A cheerless dawn was breaking as I left that dreadful place. I noticed the stains upon my boots and thought of Barbour's terrible phrase – 'reid wat shod'. And so I went to meet the Gordons returning. Grim and stern and silent they marched in, but still they held their heads high, as well became the 'Gay Gordons'. At the head of the column strode a young captain, with the purple and white ribbon of the Military Cross gleaming on his breast (a year ago he was a divinity student of the Church of Scotland), and as I listened to him speaking a last word to the men as gently as a mother putting her children to bed, there was revealed to me something more of the nobility of the men with whom I had to do.

It was Sunday morning, and as I turned away with a heavy heart I saw the grey wrack of clouds lifting in mass and rolling westwards, and a band of saffron light like the body of heaven in its clearness lay over the battlefield, where all seemed lost but honour. That night in the gloaming we held our service as usual. But, oh! the heart-breaking pathos of it all! How near the ranks stood to the drums! Five hundred of our comrades were absent. Of the twenty-five officers who had stood there a few days before, only six returned. God alone knows what I said to them, but they marched with a swinging step, as is their wont, and the pipes flung the high defiant spirit of their race to all the winds of Flanders.

Our Duty

Such are the men who have gone from this fair city by the banks of the silvery Dee. I charge you to be worthy of them. There are those here whose hearts are hungry for the lads who will never return. Do not weep over much. Let your sorrow be seasoned with a proud thanksgiving. We shall all follow them soon, and we shall find them great of soul and cleansed in the fire of a sacrifice which is sealed with the mark of Calvary. And for you and for the rest I bid you work for those who are giving all for you. You can never do too much for these men. They are worthy of all honour and loving service. And when the armies return – as return they shall (please God!) with victory – you will then perhaps be worthy to meet them on the lofty levels of magnanimity and chivalry and sacrificial endurance to which they have become habituated in this day of Armageddon; and hand in hand with them you will go forward to the new era and the fairer world which our God will give, we believe, as a recompense.

CHAPTER EIGHT

Some Survivors

AFTER such a long period of time, and with so few surviving records, it is difficult to be accurate about the strength of U Company when it embarked for France and Belgium in February of 1915. In *Students Under Arms* Alexander Rule stated – 'Out of an embarkation strength of one hundred, only one or two came through the war unwounded'. Assuming that he was working from his diary and also his memory of events some nineteen years later, it seems from other evidence that he was mistaken. As Principal of the University, Sir George Adam Smith had always taken a very keen interest in the University Company and the Gordons: not least because his eldest son George was killed at Loos with the 2nd Gordons, but also because his second son Robert – who was to be killed in 1917 – had been an enthusiastic member of U Company before accepting a commission in the regular army.

One of the surviving members of U Company, who continued to serve as an officer with the 4th Gordons, kept his Principal (who had been knighted at the onset of 1916) abreast of developments. Sir George noted that since the Battle at Hooge the fortunes of the Battalion had been less eventful, and that it had kept its place in the British line. It remained for some time at Ypres and then moved a little farther south, and regular reinforcements continued to arrive from the reserve Battalions of the Gordons in Aberdeen. In the *Review* he quoted from a letter he received in April 1916:

> The Battalion is in a good position and in excellent health and spirits. The weather is splendid and the surroundings are quite congenial. In the fighting line things are normal and the only event of importance which has affected us has been the issue of shrapnel-proof helmets. They resemble the old clerical hat, only not so wide and rather higher. On not a few occasions they have already staved off what might have been serious or even fatal head wounds. In one case the helmet actually deflected a bullet, the wearer suffering from nothing but the impact.
>
> We never forget our fallen comrades, though we say little about it. For myself, I think they are not far from us at any time, but help us yet.

Writing in the *Aberdeen University Review* in 1916, six months after the battles of Hooge and Loos, Sir George noted that of approximately 120 rank and file student and graduate members of U Company who went from Bedford to Flanders in February of 1915 only three were left in the ranks. Of the remainder some 24 had ceased to serve in the infantry, 33 had been commissioned, and 63 had been killed, wounded or invalided out of the army. He also mentioned that an additional eight officers and 27 men of the University had served in the 4th Gordons in A, B and C Companies.

After the War

The survivors of U Company returned to a different Britain. Far from Lloyd George's 'fit country for heroes to live in', it was a country where unemployment had risen from the pre-war level of just over one per cent of the population to almost ten per cent. Many of the unemployed were almost destitute and some of those in work were not much better off. Ex-servicemen without jobs, many of whom had lost limbs, tried to make a living by selling matches on street corners. The North of Scotland ethos of making sacrifices to obtain a university education seemed more sensible than ever and the returning students set to work with a renewed seriousness.

Many of the survivors were in a hurry to make up for time lost while serving their country in a thoroughly unpleasant war. One was Charles (Chatty) Donald who rose from the dizzy heights of assistant cook (to Sandy Silver) in U Company to a commission in the 5th Gordons and then became a lieutenant in the Royal Flying Corps. Donald returned to his medical studies and frequently had his leg pulled over his abilities as a cook. When asked at Bedford by his commanding officer how he knew when the spuds he was boiling in a large dixie were ready, he replied: 'you take one out and throw it against the wall, and if it sticks they're cooked.' He graduated MB ChB at Aberdeen in 1922 and became a Harley Street surgeon with posts at Great Ormond Street and the Royal Masonic Hospitals among others. In the Second World War he was consulting surgeon to the Middle East and Central Mediterranean Forces with the rank of Brigadier, and after that war he became known as one of the leading authorities in London on the surgery of the thyroid gland. He died in 1955 at the age of 59.

Medicine attracted many of the survivors of U Company who had had other ambitions before the war. Sergeant (John) Douglas McLaggan (MA 1914), who was wounded at Hooge, graduated MB ChB in 1920 at Aberdeen with distinction in his final examinations, then took two surgical fellowships in quick succession and also set off for Harley Street. Appointed to the staff of the Royal Free Hospital in 1931, he was in charge of the Ear Nose and Throat department until he retired in 1958. As an aural surgeon he attended four generations of the Royal Family up to and including Queen Elizabeth II, and he was made a KCVO in 1958. He did not forget his Scottish roots, and in reply to an old U Company friend who congratulated him on his knighthood he wrote to say that he was 'biggin a bungalow for his retirement'. McLaggan had been a very good hockey player at University and was later capped for Scotland. In his laconic entry in the *University of Aberdeen Roll of Service*, compiled in 1921, he does not go into much detail about his war service. There is no mention of being wounded at Hooge on 25 September nor of being commissioned into his own Battalion in 1916. He states simply, 'L/Cpl., U Coy., 4th Gordon Hrs., 1914' and obviously considered that to be honour enough.

The members of U Company had an abundance of talents. In the scholastic field they took many prizes, and honours degrees were gained with ease. They could speak the Doric and Gaelic, write Greek verse or polished English essays and conjugate Latin verbs – one of them was even nicknamed 'Homer'. This was Leslie McKenzie, another member of the famous and ill-fated Arts class of 1911-15 whose talents were so sadly wasted. McKenzie had gained his nickname while at Robert Gordon's College because of his great aptitude for classics. At the university he proved himself one of the best classical scholars of his year winning the Jenkins Prize in Classical Philology in 1914, before he had completed his course. Fate decreed that he should not finish his honours course, but such was his record that his Alma Mater conferred on him his MA (Hons) degree *in absentia* in March 1915. As an enthusiastic member of U Company, McKenzie had been mobilised as a full corporal at the outbreak of war and trained with them at Bedford. On New Year's day 1915 he was commissioned into the 8th Black Watch and crossed to France with them in May. Twice severely wounded, he returned to the front each time and served until he was so seriously wounded at Arras that he died on 2 April 1918.

Olympic Athlete

A number of the members of U Company were great debaters and many were fine athletes in a number of fields. One such was Arthur Spark, a son of the Reverend Robert Spark of the manse of Durris in Kincardine. Robert Spark was a Glasgow graduate and he had four children who all served in the Great War and all graduated in medicine at Aberdeen between 1917 and 1924. Three of the next Spark generation also graduated as doctors at Aberdeen between 1948 and 1951. Arthur Spark, who had joined U Company as a 15 year-old in 1909, was a medical student when he went to France in February of 1915. He was a very big man and weighed about 15 stones, and Sandy Rule remarked that he suffered his first wound when Spark fell on top of him while they were trying to get in to a front-line trench on a very dark night. Spark was wounded in May and commissioned into the 7th Gordons in July. Because of the shortage of medical officers he was sent back to his studies, and after graduating in 1917 he served as a surgeon-lieutenant in the Royal Navy. Early in the war he played for Scotland in a war-time rugby international against England. In 1924 he represented Great Britain in the Decathlon and Pentathlon in the 'Chariots of Fire' Olympic Games in Paris, and went on to represent the British Empire in America in 1928 in the Shot, Hammer and Discus. He was Lord Mayor of Stoke-on-Trent from 1945-50 and died there aged 59 in 1953.

The medical student who gave the impromptu organ recital in the roofless church at Zillebeke also returned to his studies. He was James Morrison of Aberdeen, and, as the RAMC was short of doctors, he resumed his studies after the battle at Hooge, qualifying in 1917. He went straight into the RAMC and transferred to the regular army at the war's end. Promoted to the rank of major in 1929, he served in India and Singapore and he was Assistant Director of Medical Services to the 3rd AA Division at the outbreak of the second war. His health had not been robust since his experiences in France in the Great War and in 1943 he was invalided out of the army. He retired to Grantown-on-Spey in 1945 and died there in 1967 at the age of 75.

Another sportsman who returned to his studies was Alexander Cooper the golfer. Prior to the war he was an arts student, specialising in mathematics, and he had been a keen member of U Company. He was a member of the Aberdeen Victoria and Deeside golf clubs and in 1913 had been captain-elect of the University golf club and led the University to victory in the annual Aberdeen Maitland Shield foursomes. Cooper suffered a serious penetrating chest wound in the battle at Hooge and lay dangerously ill in hospital at Étaples for some time. He made a slow recovery and was invalided out of the army to graduate MA in 1917 and MB ChB in 1921. When the Maitland Shield foursomes resumed after the war Cooper again captained the University side which retained the trophy. On that occasion he was aided by the inclusion in the second string of another war-veteran medical student, the Yorkshire-born Lieutenant William Tweddell, MC and bar, who went on to win the British Amateur Golf Championship at Hoylake in 1927. Dr Cooper became a consultant chest physician in Guildford. He retired to Dundee and died there at the age of 78 in 1973.

Beyond Aberdeen

Not all the survivors returned to their studies at Aberdeen. Frederick (Freddie) Bain from Macduff was a science student when mobilised with U Company and, after accompanying it to France, he was commissioned into the 4th Gordons in August 1915. Wounded at Hooge in September, and again one month later, he finished the war as a captain with a Military Cross. He then went to work for ICI and, after being knighted in 1945, finally became the deputy chairman and chairman-elect of the company in 1950. In that year he did become a graduate when the honorary degree of LLD was conferred on him by his old University, thus joining a distinguished élite which included his old Commander-in-Chief Field Marshal Sir Douglas Haig. Bain died in November 1950.

Alexander (Sandy) Rule, the chronicler of U Company's adventures, led a very adventurous life himself after the war a long way from his native Huntly. Rule barely survived Hooge where he was found in a trench late in the day badly wounded in the back and in the foot – he lost two toes – and suffering from shock, and he spent several periods in hospital. In later years he liked to recall that his overriding concern at the time was not if he would lose his foot, but whether he would be able to dance again. He was commissioned in January 1917 and went back to France to serve, with the 4th Gordons, until the end of the war, which he reached with the rank of captain and the Military Cross. He returned to his Alma Mater and graduated MA in 1920 and took a BSc in forestry the following year. He soon set off for Australia where he worked as a forester and travelled extensively until he returned to serve his country in the Second World War. He became an advisor to the United Nations in forestry in 1951, and when he retired in 1960 he held the post of Technical Assistance Director-General of the Forest and Timber Bureau in Canberra. Rule contributed to the literature on forestry throughout his life and wrote another successful book entitled *Forests of Australia*.

Students Under Arms

The text of *Students Under Arms* was completed in 1934 and the book was published privately by Rule who enlisted the help of Theodore Watt of the Aberdeen University Press. Five hundred copies were printed and sold out in a short period of time, although correspondence between Watt and Rule in 1946 showed that 250 unbound copies were still held by the University Press. The introduction to the book was written by the distinguished Aberdeen graduate John Malcolm Bulloch, himself a historian and newspaperman of considerable distinction. Bulloch was on the staff of Allied Newspapers, whose chairman was Lord Camrose, and he wrote to Rule in January 1935 that he;

> would be interested to know that Sir James Edmonds, the army historian, told me today at our committee meeting in the War Office of the Society for Army Historical Research, that he greatly liked your book, which he said caught the whole spirit of the great adventure. Sir James is a man of few words, and never says what he does not mean, and I confess I was very much struck with this opinion of your book from a man who knows better than anybody else what is what in the shape of war histories. He has probably read more of them than anybody in the country.

R B (Roy) Strathdee, who was associated with the University of Aberdeen Officers Training Corps from 1928, and was the commanding officer with the rank of Lieut-Colonel from 1940-47, wrote an interesting letter to Rule.

109

Dust cover of *Students Under Arms*

17 Albyn Place
Aberdeen
18 Dec 1934

My Dear Rule,

Just a line to thank you for the sheer enjoyment I experienced in reading your *Students Under Arms*. If I could afford it I would present copies to those writers who were responsible a few years ago for that spate of so-called 'war books'. Have we in the North a different make up from our brethren in the South? If not, why should our war reactions be so different, unless of course they want to convert (mostly untrue) pictures of blood and sex into money. Such would, I presume, still savour of the 'war profiteer' rather the real historian. A criticism – Sandy! I do not think your book complete without 'U' Company's Roll – i.e. at time of mobilisation. In the meantime the Compliments of the Season and all good wishes for the deserved success of your most enjoyable book.

Yours aye

R B Strathdee

110

Among many other letters of congratulation sent to Rule was one from General Sir Ian Hamilton who added a postscript to the effect that he – 'remembered as clearly as if it were yesterday the Company on parade at Bedford'. After a long and full life Alexander Rule died at Blairgowrie in 1983 at the age of 87. It was entirely fitting that at his funeral service the congregation should sing *Gaudeamus* for this staunch member of U Company and graduate who graced the name of the University of Aberdeen wherever he represented it throughout the world.

When Sandy Rule graduated MA in 1920 some of his fellow-graduates at the ceremony shouted 'give us a song, Sandy'. This was a tribute to the part he played in student activities after the Great War where he was a frequent speaker at dinners and chairman of re-unions. He also played a prominent part in Gala Week activities and was part of a large cast which, on two successive years, toured Aberdeenshire during the week performing 'A Mock Trial'. In May of 1921 this took the form of 'A Breach of Promise Case' and among the cast were Charles Donald as 'Sir Rudd Y Twister', Eric Linklater as 'Sir Wallace Tower', Guthrie Badenoch as Clerk of Court and Rule himself as 'Mr Maxim Niblick', a witness.

Sandy Rule's University badge

Rule remained a life-long diary keeper and he recorded faithfully his world-wide meetings with other Aberdeen University graduates and war-time friends from the 4th Gordons and other units. He retained a strong attachment to his fellow survivors of U Company and some of his trips to Africa, Asia and South America were financed by another survivor, Murdo Mackenzie. Mackenzie was another adventurous entrepreneur who had decided to seek fame and fortune outside Aberdeen and he set off for London where he founded Mackenzie Engineering Ltd, with himself as chairman and managing director. After a chance meeting in London in the 1940s during which he recognised Rule's expert knowledge of forestry and timber (and his contacts in the business), he employed him as a consultant and so helped to further Sandy Rule's travels about the world by ocean liner and somewhat unreliable aircraft.

Among his many papers there is a 'Field Service Post Card' sent on 14 July 1916 by his friend Sandy Gunn from Caithness – nine days before Gunn was killed at High Wood on the Somme. It was sent to Ripon where Rule was training before being commissioned, and it is addressed to 'Private J [John] Rule, L M of S of G J' and it is signed 'John Gunn'. The initials stand for 'Life member of the Society of Good Johns' and are a reference to the secret society, with its own signals, which was formed some weeks before the battle at Hooge with Gunn and Rule among the principals.

Rule's papers contain numerous references to his friends in U Company. Two of these friends were Stewart Mirrlees and Francis Rumbles, both of whom had graduated in arts in 1914. Stewart Mirrlees wrote some of the 'Letters from the Front' which appeared in *Alma Mater* and were signed with his initials 'STAM'. In a letter from Belgium on 19 April 1915 he wrote:

> Picture a convoy of heavily loaded (or laden) figures, lying in easy attitudes on the soft ease of a *pavé* road. 'Tis dark, a bullet smacks into a neighbouring tree, and a voice comes out of the darkness: – 'John, would you like a meat sandwich? Well, I haven't got one you know'.

111

1,Hyde Park Gardens,W.2.

Paddington 5104.

22nd Dec. 1934.

Dear Mr. Rule,

I have just finished your book,
"Students Under Arms" which will now form part
of my library.   Having done so, I feel
moved to write you just a line congratulating
you very warmly on the work.   You have
steered an admirable course between the com-
memoration of gallantry and any tendency towards
jingoism.   As to the style; the sense of proportion displayed and the picture on the cover I
don't think you could possibly have done better.

With all wishes for a big sale,

Believe me,

Yours sincerely,

Ian Hamilton /P.T.O.

P.S.   I remember as clearly as if it
were yesterday the company on parade at
Bedford.

A.F.A. 2042.
114/Gen. No./5248.

FIELD   SERVICE

POST CARD.

The address
only to be writ-
ten on this side.
If anything else
is added, the
post card will
be destroyed.

*Pte J. Rule
L. M. of S of G.J.,
4th Res Bn Gordon Hrs,
Ripon.*

112

Francis Rumbles was a native of Deskford in Banffshire and had been classical medallist at Fordyce Academy and a keen member of U Company at University. As a schoolboy he had been a skilful angler and an excellent shot and this practical competence led to his appointment as divisional instructor in musketry after he was invalided home from France as a result of wounds in 1915. After the war he taught at Robert Gordon's College for a time and then in 1922 he was appointed to the headmastership of the village school at Breconbeds in Dumfries-shire. There he found his life's work as a dominie in the old Scottish tradition; maintaining his own studies in the classics and mathematics, and continuing to coach his old pupils long after they had left him for senior school and university. Francis Rumbles died in 1962 at the age of 72.

Another member of the 1911 Arts class was Robert T Donald. Born in Towie, Donald graduated in arts in 1914 and was mobilised on 4 August with the Company of which he had been a member for over two years. He was one of three diarists in the Company from the 1911 Arts class and all the writers would have been well aware that keeping a diary on active service was forbidden by military law. After being slightly wounded in May 1915 he was commissioned in August into the 7th Black Watch as a 2nd Lieutenant and served in Mesopotamia and India: he finished his long war in 1919 with the rank of captain. Donald taught English at Fraserburgh Academy before being appointed principal teacher of English and History at Inverurie Academy. In Inverurie he was the originator of the Inverurie Players and he died suddenly at one of his productions in 1936 at the early age of 43. His widow Louise Donald, also an arts graduate of Aberdeen, was head of the English department at Aberdeen High School for Girls, and much later took a degree in law at the University when over seventy years of age. She was joint editor and compiler with W S Macdonald of the fourth *Roll of Graduates 1956-1970*, of the University of Aberdeen, following in the illustrious footsteps of Colonel William Johnston, Theodore Watt and John Mackintosh in that behemothic task. One of Robert Donald's sons, Sir Alan Donald, KCMG, was the British Ambassador to China from 1988-91, and in 1991 he received the degree of Doctor of Laws (*honoris causa*) from his father's Alma Mater. Another son, Robert Turner Donald, qualified in medicine at Aberdeen in 1951.

Medical Students

James Fraser, who had graduated in arts in 1914, was another who graduated with honours in medicine in 1922. The period after the Great War saw the last of the truly educated doctors. Prior to the war it was quite common for a young man or woman who intended to study medicine to take an arts degree in the first place. In his unpublished memoirs, Dr Walter Graham recalls how he had to abandon his arts course because of ill-health and continue the study of medicine after the war in the company of many of the returned veterans. Walter Graham had a long and distinguished career as a general medical practitioner in private practice in St John's Wood in London, and he put his earlier study of the classics to use when he wrote the most sensitive parts of his medical notes about his illustrious patients in Greek. Always a modest man, he did not record this fact in his memoirs, nor did he say how his poor *locum tenens* managed when confronted with medical notes written in Greek.

Graham remarked on the maturity of the veterans and their keenness to get through their examinations. In particular he recalled going to the dissecting-room at Marischal College – known to generations of medical students as going 'down the drain' – to compete with the veterans in the study of anatomy using corpses. As he put it – 'The trouble was that they were so enthusiastic about dissection that the corpses had been out for only two days, and we children who had just come out of school had to do what we could with the remains of the remains.' He also noted that when he qualified it was with what was called a 'star', but he was at pains to point out that a star meant simply that you had achieved 75% in all your final examinations in medicine, surgery and obstetrics, and was not at all like an honours degree in medicine.

James Fraser also made the point about the difficulty of getting a place at a dissecting table or a part of a body to dissect, and he attributed this to the fact that the 46 ex-servicemen students were in addition to the normal intake of youngsters from the schools. Not all the veterans completed their degrees in the post-war enthusiasm for the study of medicine. Some fell by the wayside in the heady delights of the free and unfettered life of the student body, which was in such marked contrast to the years of discipline and obedience which they had undergone in the armed forces. One student, Robert Jolly from Dundee, had been discharged from the army as a 2nd Lieutenant in the 4th Gordons. Jolly had enlisted in the Gordons as a 17 year-old in November 1914 and had joined the Battalion in Flanders in July of 1915. He served in Belgium and France continuously until he was badly gassed in December 1917. At the end of the war, in April 1919, he went up to Marischal College to study medicine with his friends, but the effects of the gas continued to trouble him and he died on 26 November 1919 at the age of 22 years. This was not an uncommon story with the empirical medicine of the day and many wounded men succumbed to the effects of their wounds; sometimes years after the war.

Gala Week

As a member of the Students' Representative Council, James Fraser was one of the students who, in 1920, founded the annual week-long Gala Week at Aberdeen. This was instituted as a result of an appeal to the university authorities from the board of directors of the Royal Infirmary at Woolmanhill to ask if students could help in raising funds for the hard-pressed voluntary hospitals. The SRC formed a committee and Gala Week began, and has continued to the present day. The shows put on by the students at His Majesty's Theatre caught the imagination of the public, and the talented veterans, among whom was the future renowned author Eric Linklater, were responsible for *Stella the Bajanella* in 1922 and *The Prince Appears* among others. Perhaps the most popular show of all was the historic *Town and Gown* which was put on in 1933. This show (and *Hitting Back* in 1949) had a poignant scene where the university sacrists played draughts while discussing the war in general and U Company's departure for Bedford in particular, and this was followed by another scene of the battlefield in September 1915 where the Company ceased to exist.

Walter Graham was one of those who studied medicine with Eric Linklater at Aberdeen and in his memoirs he recalled that period in his life.

> The medical course in Aberdeen was five years in duration and my course was from 1920-25. It was a good time to be at university because half of the class were like myself more or less one year out of school, but the other half were veterans of World War I. Some of them had decorations. They had a maturity about them and a sense of purpose which we youngsters did not have, but I think their sense of purpose and their outlook rubbed off on us a bit. One of the features of university life in those days was the hospital's Gala Week. During the Easter holidays – remember this was long before the days of the National Health Service – in the early 1920s, all sorts of efforts were made to raise money for the hospital. Concert parties were sent out, there was a week's performance of a revue usually written by Eric Linklater who was up at that time, and of whom I'll say a bit more later, and quite a bit of money was raised.

114

Sir Alexander Graham and Sir Peter Graham - the sons of Dr Walter Graham

Linklater was an extraordinary person. He was an Orcadian. He got himself into the army having lied about his age: I think he was sixteen when he went to World War I. This was a terrible war; trench warfare must have been absolutely hideous, but he didn't seem to have suffered very much in the war from any loss of wit or humour. He had a very acid wit. He used to write the libretto for this revue and the music was written by another student John Taylor, and a chap called Jim Crombie - who later became Sir James Crombie, first secretary of the Treasury or something frightfully grand - conducted the orchestra. At one of my school's [Aberdeen Grammar School] reunion dinners - I think it must have been in the 1950s or 1960s - three people were asked to the dinner at the same time. Eric Linklater who had written the script, Jimmie Crombie who had conducted the orchestra, and myself who had sung the songs.

This particular revue was called *The Prince Appears* and it really was a very good show indeed, so much so that after it was all over we were asked if we would do a potted version on the local wireless - the days of 'cat's whiskers' sets; television was still a dream. Well, we put the show over the air and about a week later Eric Linklater came up to me and pressed three guineas into my hands. 'What on earth's that for', I asked? He said, 'that's for singing on the wireless'. 'Well' said I, 'I'll never earn three guineas so easily or so pleasantly again', and I never have. Three guineas in 1924 was about a working man's weekly wage. Even today I would sing songs all day for three guineas a time but the trouble is I can't sing very much now. There's always a snag, isn't there?

115

Linklater never qualified in medicine; he never got through the second professional anatomy exam, and after a few years I should think – he probably studied medicine for four years – he went to the faculty of arts, got a first-class honours degree in English and went out to India as assistant editor to the Bombay *Times*. He later came back to Scotland and settled down as an author. Some of his early books of course, are very autobiographical and you can spot the people even though the names used in the books are not those you knew as a youngster.

Eric Linklater as a medical student in 1921

In *Fanfare For a Tin Hat*, Eric Linklater recalled his memory of graduating in arts in 1925 at Aberdeen.

The bright light of realism colours one of my last student memories. In an undistinguished year I had taken my degree and decorated it with several prizes. That gratified my mother, but when I met Professor McKerron [professor of midwifery] in Broad Street he beckoned to me from the other pavement, and as I crossed the road he shouted, 'Clever fellow, aren't you Linklater? You stay here till there's no competition left – all the good ones have gone – so you walk in and scoop the pool. Well, well, good luck to you. There's a lot of art in good timing.'

University OTC

After qualification in 1922 James Fraser took up medical practice in Aberdeen with his brother Tom who had served at Gallipoli, and as a colonel in the RAMC was awarded the DSO and made a CBE. In addition to his general practice, Thomas Fraser also held the post of assistant physician at the Aberdeen Royal Infirmary in the days long before the health service when such an appointment was on a part-time basis and quite unpaid. Tom was twenty years older than James who was somewhat in awe of his older brother, and in his memoirs, *Dr Jimmy*, he recalls that he was paid £20 a month. He could not afford a motor car on his income so he visited his patients, in all weathers, on a bicycle, although in very bad weather he was allowed to hire a taxi and solemnly warned not to spend too much time in it.

Between the two wars James Fraser continued the part-time soldiering he had begun with U Company, and from 1937-39 he was the officer commanding the medical unit of Aberdeen University OTC. Arthur Crichton, his great friend and fellow-sergeant from U Company days also continued part-time soldiering, and he commanded the infantry unit of the University OTC from 1935-40. Sandy Rule

Arthur Crichton's OTC unit inspected by Baron Meston, Chancellor of the University

mentions him frequently in his diary as 'Crichty', and notes that it was Crichton who, with his vest-pocket Kodak, took the photographs of some members of the Company on the train in France and in the vinery of the *Grapperies du Nord* at Bailleul. In the second war James Fraser again served throughout and mainly in India where, as a Lieut-Colonel he was a specialist in command of the medical division of a general hospital. He returned to his very successful practice in Aberdeen which he carried on single-handedly after his brother's death. He died aged 85 in 1979.

Arthur Crichton had, like James Fraser, suffered a wound in the thigh which had involved the bone, but he also managed to return to serve as an officer in the 4th Gordons. Crichton took a BSc in 1920 to add to his MA of 1914 and became a founder-member of the staff of the Rowett Research Institute in Aberdeen where he was an associate of another very distinguished war veteran, [Sir] John Boyd Orr, DSO, MC, FRS. Orr, a Glasgow graduate, had been on the staff of Aberdeen University as a researcher in animal nutrition before the Great War. During the war he had the unusual record of serving first as medical officer to the 1st

Eric Linklater, Unknown, Arthur Crichton, H J Butchart, James Fraser at an OTC camp in the early 1920s

117

Sherwood Foresters, with whom he won both his DSO and MC, and subsequently as a surgeon in the Royal Navy aboard HMS *Furious*. His work as a nutritionist made him world famous and he became Director-General of the World Food and Agricultural Organisation from 1945-48. He was created a Baron in 1949 and won the Nobel Prize in the same year. Arthur Crichton also had a distinguished career as Head of the Duthie Experimental farm, deputy Principal of the North of Scotland College of Agriculture, and later manager of the Weasenham farm complex, one of the largest agricultural combines in Britain. When he died aged 77 in 1972, his obituary in the *Aberdeen University Review* was contributed by his old friend James Fraser.

With Honours

It has been said that the members of U Company gained honours degrees with ease, and a glance at the appendix will show that at least 30 such degrees were awarded, both before and after the war, to those who embarked on the 'great adventure' in February of 1915. The 22 year old Charles Reid already had one honours degree when he sailed with his friends to France but that did not help him to rise above the rank of private. Reid was also a member of the 1911 Arts class, and when he resumed his studies in 1916 he applied himself again to considerable effect. After taking a BSc with special distinction in 1916 he graduated MB ChB with honours in 1917 and was commissioned into the RAMC and again served in France with various units from 1917 until 1920. Reid was a young man in a hurry and, after taking the DPH at Cambridge in 1921, he acquired yet another honours degree when he graduated MD at Aberdeen. He followed that with the degree of DSc in 1927 and from 1929-32 occupied the chair of Physiology in the Prince of Wales' Medical College at the University of Patna in India. Twelve years as Reader in Physiology at the University of London was followed by four years as Professor at Cairo University; and finally he was the World Health Organisation Professor of Physiology in Karachi from 1952-57. It was fitting that this distinguished graduate should join the other eight members of U Company who were asked to provide information on their careers for *Who's Who*, but curious that his own University of Aberdeen did not see fit to honour him with an honorary degree.

After three spells in action in France, Edward Knox recovered from his wounds and graduated MA and went on to become head of the history department at Kelso High School. In March of 1915 Sandy Rule confided to his diary that Sandy Skinner had pinched a whole jar of rum for 16 platoon, and after a rather splendid evening 'Knoxie gave the longest and best sustained impression of Professor Grierson to date'. His rendering of a favourite of Grierson's:

Lente, lente, currite noctis equi
Timor mortis conturbat me

left them all rather thoughtful, and they were 'transported in imagination back to a familiar class-room; the war was temporarily forgotten'. The second line – 'The fear of death overwhelms me' – must have seemed peculiarly apposite to their circumstances at the time. Edward Knox was one of a band of four brilliant brothers whose father was a book-binder in Aberdeen. Knox's own academic career got off to a rather uncertain start as he matriculated in medicine in 1910-11 when he joined U Company, in arts from 1911-14, and in the post-war enthusiasm for medicine he began again as a medical student in 1919. He eventually graduated MA in 1925.

His eldest brother James graduated MA with first class honours in classics in 1897, and after serving as a lieutenant with the 4th Gordons in France he returned to teaching and the headmastership of Ruthrieston Intermediate School in Aberdeen in 1926. Of his other brothers, Alexander Knox also took an MA with honours and served as a corporal with the 4th Gordons, being taken prisoner in 1918. He also returned to his teaching post at Mackie Academy in Stonehaven, and was rector there from 1927-49. Robert Knox graduated MA in 1910 with first class honours in English and joined U Company at the outbreak of war. He served as a captain with the 3rd Gordons in France and was taken prisoner by the Germans in 1918. After the war he graduated BA with first class honours at Oxford University and was Professor of English Literature at the University of Toronto from 1920-58.

Down the years

Had this been a larger history of U Company from its beginnings in 1898 up to 1915, it would have included the fact that by far the greatest proportion of the Company's membership over the years entered the teaching profession. But teaching was not so popular after the Great War and a high proportion (30 in all) of the survivors of the wartime Company qualified in medicine. By the 1930s the graduate list of all who had served with U Company since its formation included 13 professors and two university vice-chancellors, and, although he did not name them, Rule claimed two ex-privates as a sheriff and a judge. Of the 35 who had entered the church one had become a bishop. The bishop was an old colour-sergeant of U Company, Ernest Danson MA, DD, who was bishop of Sarawak before being enthroned in Edinburgh in 1939. A full platoon of U Company was said to be supporting the Empire, with one a knight in the Indian Civil Service and one a member of Parliament, and well over a hundred had followed the old adage to 'haud sooth, Davie' and had headed south to England as doctors, chemists, botanists, agriculturists and businessmen.

It is unlikely that the British army will see a unit like the University Company of the 4th Battalion of the Gordon Highlanders again. Not only have the Gordon Highlanders ceased to be, but the conditions which allowed this body of remarkable young men to serve as a unit no longer exist. The world is a different place and the simple and unquestioning patriotism of 1914, allied to a practical and often intense religious conviction, is not now present in Scotland or Britain as a whole. The lack of communication between the commanders and the fighting men in the field now seems a strange phenomenon to a generation which has grown up in an age of communications where television reports can be received instantly by satellite from distant continents many thousands of miles apart. With television cameras bringing the carnage into the nation's sitting rooms night after night, the prospect of another long drawn-out and large-scale war like the first Great War seems remote.

For a time after the Great War there was a certain hankering among its survivors for a return of the comradeship which had sustained them through the most terrible experiences, and friendships formed in and out of battle were not lightly broken. Perhaps Alexander Rule articulated their feelings when he wrote in the *Aberdeen University Review* in 1935 that 'however sere and yellow they were, they were still the boys of the old brigade, who would all give a lot to march once again to the rhythm of a student chorus, as mere privates of the line'.

EPILOGUE

The author has a particularly poignant memento of the battle of Hooge in the form of a copy of the *Daily Sketch* of Monday 15 November 1915. On the back page there is 'a pretty photograph of home life which was found in the trenches after the battle of Loos.' The original was thought to have been found in the tunic pocket of a slain member of U Company – and the photograph was taken in the garden of Walter Graham's residence at 35 Belvidere Street, Aberdeen. It pictures the author's mother, before her marriage, with her friend Alix Graham and Alix's brother, the then 13 year-old [Dr] Walter Graham. At the bottom of a page of similar pictures, the caption referring to this picture states:

> It seems but yesterday we sat in the garden in the quietude of a Sunday afternoon and were photographed by Cousin Bill after dinner. This might easily be the extract from a letter accompanying the picture in the centre of the top row of this page. But it brings up memories of war – not of peace. It is only one of the pictures of home life found at the front and sent to the *Daily Sketch*, the link between the fighting man and his friends at home.

The author's mother, Walter Graham and Alix Graham in June 1915

Haig's First Army of six divisions carried out the attack at Loos, and it included five Gordon battalions – the 9th, 10th, 2nd, 6th and 8th. The author's mother and Alix Graham knew a number of young men in U Company of the 4th Gordons (known as the 'City of Aberdeen battalion') who were occupied at Hooge, and it was believed that the photograph was taken from the tunic pocket of a friend who had been killed at Hooge, and not at Loos. How it got to the newspaper, nobody had the least idea.

Page 16.—DAILY SKETCH, MONDAY, NOVEMBER 15, 1915.

DID YOU GET YOUR SUNDAY HERALD?

IF NOT, ORDER IT TO-DAY FROM YOUR NEWSAGENT

DAILY SKETCH.

Exclusively designed by our own artists, cut and explained by experts—*Daily Sketch* paper patterns. 7d. post free. See Page 15.

LONDON: Shoe Lane, E.C.   MANCHESTER: Withy Grove.
Telephones—8 Lines—Editorial and Publishing—Holborn 6512.

BRITAIN'S BEST PICTURE PAPER.

THE SUNDAY AFTERNOON: HOW SCENES OF YESTERDAY ARE RECALLED AT THE BATTLE-FRONT

The owner of this and others was an officer of a Hampshire Regiment serving in Gallipoli.

This pretty photograph of home life was found in the trenches after the battle of Loos.

The Inniskilling who sent this thinks it belonged to one of the K.O.S.Bs.

An Irish Guardsman has sent this from France, where he found it after a battle.

The gallant death of the sergeant-major who owned this picture is told on another page. He belonged to the Royal Engineers.

A happy picture found in France by a member of the East Surreys.

"Joe and Willie's dog." A relic from the Ypres district.

Picked up with a piece of white heather by an Australian in Gallipoli.

"Give this to my girl; she lives at ——, Hampstead."

Probably the owner is in the Staffordshire Territorials.

"It seems but yesterday we sat in the garden in the quietude of a Sunday afternoon and were photographed by Cousin Bill after dinner." . . . This might easily be the extract from a letter accompanying the picture in the centre of the top row of this page. But it brings up memories of war—not of peace. It is only one of the pictures of home-life found at the front and sent to the *Daily Sketch*, the link between the fighting man and his friends at home.

Printed and Published for the Proprietors of the LONDON PUBLISHING CO., LTD., by E. HULTON and CO., LTD., London and Manchester.—MONDAY, NOVEMBER 15, 1915.

Alma Mater's Envoi

In 1916, one year after Hooge, *Alma Mater* produced its own inimitable epitaph for U Company.

Memories of 'U'

Gaily we've marched on the winding road,
Singing a rollicking air;
Laughingly tumbled through hedge and copse,
In England's fields so fair;
Boyishly pranked in billet and out,
Never a cloud in the sky;
Jestingly talked of the task in front,
Gradually drawing nigh.

Plodding along on the cobble stones,
Singing the old refrain;
Ploughing the path to a Flanders trench,
Mud, and bullets, and rain;
Eating and sleeping, fighting and digging,
Our home the sandbagged wall;
Sharing our labours, our joys, our woes,
Comrades and brothers all.

O, many sleep on in the little farmyard,
Nigh Kemmel's wooded hill,
And many more by the Menin Road,
Are lying cold and still.

Soft be your pillows, O brothers dear,
Heavenward your spirits soar,
Comrades in billet, in field, in trench,
Our comrades – evermore.

APPENDIX A

In 1919 W & W Lindsay of Aberdeen produced a publication for the Students' Representative Council. This was *Alma Mater Memorial Number Vol II*. The fly-leaf carried the single line – 'They carry back bright to the Coiner the mintage of man' – and the editorial note reads as follows:

In the Autumn of 1916 the first Memorial Number of *Alma Mater* appeared, commemorating the names and lives of 108 men who had fallen; and it is now followed by a second, which it has become possible to make the last.

In sending out this Memorial Number the Editors are deeply conscious that such a book is and must remain pitifully inadequate to the facts and the experience which it contains, and to the feeling and intention that lie behind it. Only in the course of preparation did we ourselves come to realise how great and how impossible was our task, as we learned more and more fully what the loss of these men means to their relatives and friends, to their Alma Mater, to us who, like them, are her children, and to the world in which their work was not yet done. But that was inevitable, and perhaps there is no need for self-reproach.

"We cannot for forgetfulness forego the reverence due to them...."

Faulty as it is, this record of their lives and of what manner of men they were should secure for them in the hearts and minds of the students of their University, now and in the years to come, a more intimate regard and a more enduring memory. It is in this hope that we publish it now.

The time has not yet come when we can see this experience through which our generation has passed as it really is. It is too near, too poignant and personal. We remember in these days that sorrowful saying of Pericles when the youth of Athens had been destroyed in a terrible war;– "It is as if the spring had been taken from the year;" and, far more in our day than then, it is against this sense of unnatural and irreparable loss that the world is finding the lighter consolations and the easier philosophies of no avail. This, it may be, was needed to produce a positive desire for a way of life that will make such another experience forever impossible. To the task of making the world anew their death has given the needed consecration.

Of Our Dead themselves we would not here speak. To those of us who knew them, the years in front – emptier than we had looked for – will yet hold the memory of glad companionships; to all their fellow-students now and down the long ages, the knowledge of what these men have been and done will go to the enrichment of those things which make a University a place of visions and of vows. They have been taken out from beneath the sun, but their feet are set at last in a large place; and to them, in all love and reverence, we dedicate this Book.

The Editors

APPENDIX B

Members of U Company of the 4th Gordons with their ranks when they sailed to join the BEF in February 1915. Some members of the Company who, for various reasons, did not embark with the main body but re-joined later, are also included.

Sergeant Alexander Allardyce
D/B 22 November 1884 - Rothiemay
MA 1904 BL 1907
U Company 1904-10
France – February - July 1915
Killed at Hooge 20 July 1915 aged 30
Solicitor with Hunter and Gordon, Aberdeen

Private James Anderson
D/B 29 April 1892 - Portknockie
Arts 1911-14
U Company 1913-14
France – February - September 1915
Member of the sniper section
Killed at Hooge 25 September 1915 aged 23

Private James S Anderson
D/B 3 December 1891 - Aberdeen
MA 1914
U Company 1910-14
France – February - September 1915
Commd Gordons June 1917
Final rank 2nd Lieutenant
MA (Hons) 1919 MB ChB (Dist) 1921
    DPH 1922 MD (Hons) 1923
Physician St George's Hospital, London
Retired 1956

Private William Anderson
D/B 6 January 1895 - Peterhead
Medicine 1913-14
U Company 1914
France – February - June 1915
Wounded Flanders June 1915
Resumed studies MB ChB 1919
General practice in Wolleston
Died 1973 aged 78

Lance-Corporal William A Asher
D/B 25 August 1893 - Elgin
Arts 1912-14
U Company 1912-14
France – February 1915 - September 1916
Commd HLI 1917 Final rank Lieutenant
MA 1919
Education Officer 1st Gordons 1919 Instructor
    Army School of Education 1926
Indian Military Academy Dehra Dun 1932
Deputy Director Military Education India
    1946-48
Final rank Colonel

Private Frederick W Bain
D/B 22 March 1889 - Macduff
Science 1912-13
U Company 1910-14
France – February 1915 - January 1916
Commd 4th Gordons August 1915
Wounded at Hooge 25 September 1915
Final rank Captain - MC 1916
Deputy Chairman ICI
Knighted 1945 Hon LLD Aberdeen 1950
Entry in *Who's Who*
Died 1950 aged 61

Private Arthur M Barron
D/B 17 August 1894 - New Byth
Arts 1913-14
U Company 1913-14
France – February - September 1915
Wounded in April and at Hooge 25 Sept. 1915
Commd 7th Gordons October 1915
Final rank Lieutenant - MC 1917
Transferred RAF February 1918
MB ChB 1924 MD 1932
Consultant Physician Poole General Hospital
    1927
Died 1979 aged 85

Private Douglas D Booth
D/B
Agriculture 1913-14
U Company 1914
France – February - September 1915
Wounded in April and at Hooge 25 Sept.1915

Private John L Booth
D/B 10 September 1892 - Aberdeen
MA (Hons) 1914
U Company 1911-14
France – February 1915 - April 1918
Commd 2nd Seaforths 1915 - MC 1916
Final rank Lt-Colonel
Commanding Officer of his Battalion - a unique
    record for a Territorial in a line regiment
Killed at La Bassée 18 April 1918 aged 25

Private Evan M Burns
D/B 9 December 1891 - Kiltarlity
MA 1914
U Company 1911-14
France – February - November 1915
Commd RE March 1916 Final rank Captain
Regular commission 1920 with Royal Corps of
    Signals
Died 1956 aged 64

Sergeant George M Calder
D/B 29 May 1891 - Edinkillie
MA (Posth) 1915 Arts and Medicine 1910-14
U Company 1911-14
France – February - March and July - Sept. 1915
Commd 8th Seaforth Highlanders March 1915
Killed at Loos 25 September 1915 aged 24
One of two members of U Company to be
    awarded a posthumous MA

2nd Lieutenant Ian A Clarke
D/B 23 June 1890 - Aberdeen
MA 1911 BSc 1912
U Company 1908-14
France – February - September 1915 and 1918
Wounded 16 June 1915
Final rank Major 4th Gordons
BA (Oxon) 1919
Forestry Commission 1920-22
Housemaster Stowe School, Bucks 1923-39
Died 1939 aged 49

Private Frederick A Conner
D/B 20 February 1895 - Aberdeen
Agriculture 1913-14
U Company 1913-14
France – February 1915 - July 1916
Commd 2nd Seaforths August 1915
Final rank 2nd Lieutenant
Killed on the Somme 1 July 1916 aged 21

Private Alexander Cooper
D/B 27 September 1894 - West Cults
Arts 1912-14
U Company 1913-14
France – February - October 1915
Wounded in June and at Hooge 25 Sept.1915
Resumed studies MA 1917 MB ChB 1921
Captain University Golf Club 1913
Senior assistant MO Brompton Hospital 1924
Consultant Chest Physician Guildford
Died 1973 aged 78

Private Harold H Corner
D/B 13 August 1896 - Inverness
Agriculture 1913-14
U Company 1914
France – February - June 1915
Wounded - Lost an eye when a sniper and
    discharged
Resumed studies BSc 1919
PhD 1938 OBE 1957
Agriculture Adviser Roxburgh 1941-61
Died 1979 aged 82

Private William Corner
D/B 25 November 1893 - Inverness
Medicine 1912-14
U Company 1914
France – February - September 1915
Resumed studies MB ChB 1916
Commd RAMC 1916 Final rank Captain
OBE (Mil) April 1919
MD 1924 DTM & H (London) 1925
Civil surgeon Iraq Health Service until 1929
General practice in Hove from 1930
Died 1981 aged 87

Private Alexander H Craig
D/B 6 June 1893 - Willesden, London
Medicine 1910-14
U Company 1910-14
France – February - September 1915
Resumed studies MB ChB 1916
Commd RAMC August 1916
Final rank Captain
After private practice in London he joined the
    Indian Medical Service. Mentioned in
    Dispatches North West Frontier between the
    wars. 1939-45 on active service in India, Iraq
    and Burma. Final rank Brigadier
Died 1961 aged 67

Private Thomas Cranston
D/B 9 February 1891 - Edinkillie
MA 1912
U Company 1912-14
France – March- May 1915, May 1916- 19
Wounded May 1915
Commd RE 1917 Final rank Lieutenant
MBE (Mil) 1919
Tax Inspector Glasgow, Aberdeen and Galashiels
Died 1966 aged 75

Corporal Arthur Crichton
D/B 24 September 1894 - Alford
MA 1914
U Company 1912-14
France – February - October 1915
Wounded in May and at Hooge 25 Sept.1915
Commd 4th Gordons 1918
Final rank 2nd Lieutenant
BSc 1920 On staff Rowett Research Institute
OC University OTC 1935-40
Deputy Principal North of Scotland Agricultural
    College 1948
Manager Weasenham Farm Complex 1951
University Blue in swimming and football
Died 1972 aged 77

Private David W Crichton
D/B 10 October 1896 - Banchory
Agriculture 1913-14
U Company 1914
France – February - May 1915
Killed near Ypres 7 May 1915 aged 18

Private James O Cruickshank
D/B 17 August 1895 - Brechin
Arts and Science 1913-14
U Company 1913-14
France – February - April 1915
Second member of U Company to be killed
Killed by sniper at Wytschaete 15 April 1915
    aged 19

Lance-Corporal Marianus A Cumming
D/B 9 December 1891 - Strichen
MA 1912
U Company 1910-14
France – February - June 1915
Schoolmaster at Kemnay before re-joining U
    Company
Killed 13 June 1915 aged 23

Private Robert Davidson
D/B 20 October 1894 - Ellon
Arts 1913-14
U Company 1913-14
France – February 1915 - July 1916
Wounded July 1916
Commd 1st Gordons 26 June 1918
Final rank 2nd Lieutenant
MB ChB 1923
General practice in Nottingham

Private Robert Dawson
D/B 7 November 1892 - Aberdeen
MA 1914
U Company 1914
France – February 1915 - April 1918
Final rank Sergeant
MB ChB 1921 MD 1932
General practice Middleton-in-Teesdale 1923-63
Died 1987 aged 94

Private Charles Donald
D/B 14 February 1896 - Aberdeen
Medicine 1913-14
U Company 1913-14
France – February - September 1915
Commd 5th Gordons Oct 1915
Final rank Lieutenant
Transferred RFC (RAF) 1917
MB ChB 1922 FRCS 1925 ChM 1930
Posts at the London and Gt Ormond Street
    Hospitals
WW2 Brigadier Consulting Surgeon ME Forces
OBE 1944
Authority on thyroid surgery - Entry in *Who's
    Who*
Died 1955 aged 59

Sergeant Robert Donald
D/B 3 May 1895 - Peterculter
Arts and Divinity 1913-14
U Company 1913-14
France – February 1915 - June 1916
A member of the sniper and intelligence section
Chosen profession was the church
Killed at Vimy Ridge 9 June 1916 aged 21

Private Robert T Donald
D/B 20 December 1892 - Towie
MA 1914
U Company 1912-14
France – February - May 1915
Wounded May 1915
Commd 7th Black Watch August 1915
Served in India and Mesopotamia
Final rank Captain
Head of English Department Inverurie Academy
The originator of 'The Inverurie Players'
Died 1936 aged 43

Private William Donald
D/B 2 July 1893 - Marnoch
Arts 1912-14
U Company 1914
France – February - September 1915
Wounded on two occasions
Killed at Hooge 25 September 1915 aged 22

Private Alexander Donaldson
D/B 16 March 1894 - Fordyce
Arts 1912-14
U Company 1912-14
France – February 1915 - August 1916
Wounded at Hooge 25 September 1915
1916 - POW in Germany for two years
MA 1920 MB ChB 1924
General practice in Stoke-on-Trent and
    Cumberland
Died 1939 aged 45

Sergeant Alexander D Duncan
D/B 23 September 1893 - Ellon
MA 1914 Divinity student
U Company 1911-14
France – February - June 1915
Wounded at Hooge 17 June 1915
Died at Wimereux 25 June 1915 aged 21

Private James Durward
D/B 3 December 1892 - Banchory-Ternan
Arts 1911-14
U Company 1914
France – February 1915 - March 1919
Commd RE 1917 Final rank Captain
MA (Hons) 1919
Director Iraq Meteorological Services 1937-40
Order of Rafidain Iraq 1940
Deputy Director Meteorolog. Services UK 1948
CMG 1953 - Entry in *Who's Who*
Died 1971 aged 79

Private Andrew M Duthie

D/B 7 December 1895 - Fraserburgh
Arts 1914
U Company 1914
France – February - April 1915
Wounded April 1915
Commd 11th Gordons July 1915
France 1917-18 Final rank Captain
DSO 1917 MC 1918
MA 1920 MB ChB (Hons) 1924 MD 1929
Consultant Obstetrician Chesterfield 1948
Died 1981 aged 85

Private George Ewen

D/B 3 December 1892 - Monquhitter
Medicine 1911-14
U Company 1912-14
France – February - September 1915
Resumed studies MB ChB 1916
Commd RAMC August 1916
Final rank Captain
Served in Salonica and Russia
General practice in County Durham
Died 1960 aged 67

Private John B Ewen

D/B 21 February 1893 - Aberdeen
MA (Hons) 1914
U Company 1914
France – March - September 1915
Secretary of University Athletic Association
Appointment with Health Insurance
    Commission for Wales which he was to take
    up after the war
Killed at Hooge 25 September 1915 aged 22

Lance-Corporal Alexander Findlater

D/B 1 April 1896 - Edinburgh
Arts 1913-14
U Company 1914
France – February - September 1915
Dux of Fordyce Academy
Nephew of Piper Findlater of the Gordons who
    won the VC at Dargai
Killed at Hooge 25 September 1915 aged 19

Private James C Forbes

D/B 23 February 1894 - Fordyce
Agriculture 1911-14
U Company 1911-14
France – February - June 1915
Killed at Hooge 17 June 1915 aged 21

Private John Forbes

D/B 28 May 1891 - Fordyce
MA (Hons) 1912
U Company 1915
France – March - September 1915
Final rank CQMS
Teacher at Fordyce, Dufftown and Fraserburgh
Headmaster at Kintore - MBE 1931
Died 1956 aged 65

Sergeant John K Forbes

D/B 12 April 1883 - Aberdeen
MA 1905 Divinity student 1912-14
U Company 1914
France – February - September 1915
Teacher at Rathven School, Buckie before
    entering the Aberdeen United Free Church
    College in 1912
Student and Sniper Sergeant written by his friends
    after his death in action
Killed at Hooge 25 September 1915 aged 32

Private Robert A D Forrest

D/B 21 February 1893 - Leytonstone
MA (Hons) 1914
U Company 1910-14
France – February - December 1915
Commd 11th Gordons 1916
Final rank Lieutenant
Served with King's African Rifles 1917-18
Hong Kong Civil Service 1919 Postmaster-
    General, Chief Magistrate then Secretary for
    Chinese Affairs
Lecturer in Oriental Languages London Univ.
Author of a standard textbook on Chinese
    Language
Died 1977 aged 83

Lance-Corporal Andrew T Fowlie

D/B 9 July 1888 - Strichen
UDA NDip Agr 1909 NDD 1910
U Company 1914
France – February - June 1915
Lecturer in Agriculture for Inverness and Ross
    and Cromarty 1909-12
County Organiser for North of Scotland College
    of Agriculture in Orkney 1912
Killed at Hooge 16 June 1915 aged 26

Corporal James F Fraser

D/B 14 March 1893 - Newmachar
MA 1914
U Company 1910-14
France – February - September 1915
Commd 2nd Argyll and Sutherland Highlanders
    August 1915
Final rank Lieutenant
Wounded at Loos 25 September 1915
MB ChB (Hons) 1922
General practice Aberdeen 1923
OC Aberdeen Univ. OTC (Med Unit) 1937-39
WW2 India 1940-45 Medical Specialist i\c
    Medical Division of General Hospital
Colonel Commanding 5th Scottish General
    Hospital 1946-51
Died 1979 aged 85

Private Albert Gammie
D/B 12 May 1895 - Turriff
Arts 1913-14
U Company 1914
France – February - September 1915
Wounded at Hooge 25 September 1915
Commd Royal Tank Corps 1917
Final rank 2nd Lieutenant
Died 1940 aged 45

Private Donald J Garden
D/B 20 November 1895 - Skye
Arts 1913-14
U Company 1914
France – February - September 1915
Wounded June 1915
MA 1920 BComm 1921 PhD (Manch)
Lecturer at Manchester Technology College
Died 1943 aged 47

Corporal Charles J D Gordon
D/B 29 January 1896 - Fearn
Medicine 1913-14
U Company 1913-14
France – February - September 1915
Wounded at Hooge 25 September 1915
Killed at High Wood, Somme 23 July 1916
    aged 20

Private Robert P Gordon
D/B 5 August 1895 - Kennethmont
Arts 1912-14
U Company 1912-14
France – February - June 1915
Awarded NCOs Proficiency Certificate
Killed at Hooge 17 June 1915 aged 19

Private John Gow
D/B 17 April 1890 - Glasgow
MA (Hons) 1913
U Company 1914
France – February - September 1915
Wounded at Hooge 25 September 1915
Principal Teacher of Mathematics Kirkwall
    Grammar School 1914-51

Private James Grieve
D/B 16 April 1896 - Gamrie, Banffshire
Arts and Medicine 1914
U Company - joined with reinforcing draft
France – 1-30 September 1915
Wounded at Hooge 25 September 1915
In hospital October 1915 - August 1916
Resumed studies MA 1918 MB ChB 1922
    DMRE (Camb) 1931
Radiologist at Burnley in Lancashire from 1931
Died 1986 aged 90

Private Alexander J Gunn
D/B 5 February 1895 - Halkirk, Caithness
Medicine 1913-14
U Company 1913-14
France – February - September 1915
Recommended for DCM 16 June 1915
Wounded at Hooge 25 September 1915
Final rank Sergeant
Killed at High Wood, Somme 23 July 1916
    aged 21

Corporal William S Haig
D/B 6 November 1892 - Lonmay
MA 1914 Divinity student
U Company 1911-14
France – February - September 1915
A member of the original Robert Gordon's
    College section of the 4th Gordons in 1910
    Transferred to U Company in 1911
Killed at Hooge 25 September 1915 aged 22

Private Arthur J Hawes
D/B 9 May 1894 - Aberdeen
Medicine 1911-14
U Company 1911-14
France – February - May 1915
Wounded May 1915
Resumed studies MB ChB 1916 DPH
Commd RAMC 1916
Final rank Captain - MC 1917
General practice in Cambridge, Norfolk and
    London
Died 1974 aged 80

Lieutenant Alexander R Henderson
D/B 8 November 1888 - Aberdeen
MA 1911
U Company 1907-12
Colour-Sergeant 1911 Commd 4th Gordons
    1914
France – February - September 1915
Killed at Hooge 25 September 1915 aged 26
Teacher at Aboyne School and well-known
    footballer and captain of St Ronald Cricket
    Club

Private Alexander C Hill
D/B 17 October 1895 - Aberdeen
Arts and Medicine 1912-14
U Company 1912-14
France – February - September 1915
Wounded at Hooge 25 September 1915
Resumed studies MA 1916 MB ChB 1918
Commd RAMC 1918
Final rank Captain
General practice in London
Died 1967 aged 72

Captain Andrew D Hopkinson
D/B 30 November 1888 - St Leonards-on-Sea
BSc 1911
U Company 1911-14
Commd 4th Gordons August 1914
France – February - June 1915 and 1917-19
Final rank Captain
Lecturer at Royal Agric. College Cirencester
Forestry Commission from 1919 - OBE
Died 1969 aged 80

Private George G Jamieson
D/B 13 April 1894 - Elgin
Arts 1911-14
U Company 1913-14
France – February - September 1915
Wounded at Hooge 25 September 1915
MA (Hons) 1920
Classics Master Helensburgh and Banff
    Academies
1924-37 Rector Mortlach School Dufftown
    1937-45
Died 1973 aged 79

Private Henry W Johnston
D/B 25 February 1890 - Aberdeen
MA 1911
U Company 1909-14
France – March - May 1915
Wounded May 1915
Commd 4th Gordons August 1915
Final rank Major
MC 1918
Head of Modern Languages Alloa Academy
    1929-44
Headmaster Clackmannan School until 1955
WW2 Colonel Commanding Army Cadet Force
Died 1974 aged 83

Private William R Kennedy
D/B 8 March 1896 - Carradale
Medicine 1914
U Company 1914
France – February - September 1915
Recommended DCM for conspicuous bravery
Commd 2nd Argyll and Sutherland Highlanders
    August 1915
Killed at Loos 25 September 1915 aged 19

Private Daniel Kerrin
D/B 22 February 1896 - Parr, Lancashire
Arts 1913-14
U Company 1912-14
France – February - June 1915
Commd 5th The King's Liverpool Regt.1916
Final rank Lieutenant
MA (Hons) 1921
English teacher at Larbert 1922
Principal Intermediate Coll. Allahabad 1926-48
English teacher Ayr 1957-61
Emigrated to South Africa
Died 1982 aged 86

Private John F Knowles
D/B 26 February 1891 - Aberdeen
MA 1912 Divinity student
U Company 1910-14
France – February - May 1915
Killed by a sniper near Ypres 5 May 1915
    aged 24

Private Edward W Knox
D/B 22 April 1890 - Aberdeen
Arts and Medicine 1910-14
U Company 1911-14
France – February - June 1915 and Oct. 1916-17
Wounded June 1915
Commd 29 August 1916 Final rank Lieutenant
MA 1925
Head of History Department Kelso High School
One of four brilliant brothers whose father was
    a book-binder in Aberdeen
Died 1962 aged 72

Private John G Lamb
D/B 16 July 1892 - Peterhead
MA 1913 BSc 1914
U Company 1910-14
France – February - October 1915
Commd RE 1916 Final rank Captain
Teacher of Maths, Science and Agric. 1921-37
Inspector of Schools until 1957
Died 1978 aged 86

Private Frederick W Law
D/B 13 March 1890 - Aberdeen
MA 1912 BSc 1912
U Company 1908-12
France – February - July 1915
Commd September 1915 Final rank Captain
Founded Rocklands Nursery at Cults
Secretary of 1908-12 Arts Class all his life
Died 1970 aged 80

Private William M Ledingham
D/B 3 November 1895 - Boyndie
Science 1913-14
U Company 1914
France – February 1915 - March 1916
Commd Gordons 1916 Final rank Lieutenant
MB ChB 1923
General practice in Stoke-on-Trent
Died 1973 aged 77

Private Douglas W M Leith
D/B 10 February 1892 - Old Meldrum
MA 1913 BSc 1914
U Company 1914
France – February - Aug. 1915 and Jan. 1916-18
Commd 4th Gordons August 1915
Final rank Lieutenant - MC 1918
Killed at Beaumez-les-Cambrai 21 March 1918
    aged 26

Private James D Leslie
D/B 2 July 1894 - Macduff
Arts 1912-14
U Company 1914
France – February - September 1915
Wounded April 1915 Commd 6th Gordons 1916
Final rank Captain - MC 1919

Sergeant George Low
D/B 20 January 1892 - Dyce
MA (Hons) 1914
U Company 1910-14
France – February - September 1915
Musketry instructor at Bedford
Commd 2nd Lieutenant 4th Gordons Aug. 1915
Killed at Hooge 25 September 1915 aged 23

Private Harry Lyon
D/B 2 February 1893 - Aberdeen
Arts and Medicine 1912-14
U Company 1914
France – February - June 1915
Killed at Hooge 16 June 1915 aged 22

Private Alexander Macaulay
D/B 31 July 1890 - Uig
Arts 1913-14
U Company 1911-14
France – February - April 1915
Wounded April 1915
Commd 4th Seaforth Highlanders August 1915
Final rank Captain - MC 1918
MA 1922
Teacher Cowdenbeath and St Andrews 1923-57
Died 1962 aged 72

Private John A McCombie
D/B 22 May 1895 - Newhills
Medicine 1913-14
U Company 1913-14
France – February 1915 - July 1916
Medical orderly to 4th Gordons 1915
Final rank Sergeant - promoted in the field
Killed on the Somme 25 July 1916 aged 21

Private Isaac H MacIver
D/B 22 February 1893 - Lochcarron
Science 1913-14
U Company 1912-14
France – February - May 1915
Wounded April 1915
Commd 4th Seaforth Highlanders August 1915
Final rank Captain

Lance-Corporal Murdo MacIver
D/B 3 June 1890 - Coll, Stornoway
Arts and Agriculture 1911-14
U Company 1911-14
France – February - June 1915
Killed near Ypres 19 June 1915 aged 25

Corporal Keith Mackay
D/B 3 March 1895 - Aberdeen
MA (Posth) 1915 Arts and Medicine 1912-14
U Company 1911-14
France – February - April 1915
Wounded near Kemmel
Died at Bailleul 28 April 1915 aged 20
Awarded posthumous MA - an unusual honour

Private Donald MacKenzie
D/B 30 August 1892 - Dingwall
MA (Hons) 1913
U Company 1914
France – February - September 1915
Commd RE 1917
Final rank 2nd Lieutenant - MM 1917
Head Classics Master Rothesay Acad. 1913-14
Classics Master Robert Gordon's College 1919
Appointed Home Civil Service (Class 1) 1920
Surveyor GPO - CBE

Private Murdo Mackenzie
D/B 27 August 1894 - Aultbea, Ross-shire
Arts 1911-14
U Company 1912-14
France – February - September 1915
Commd October 1915
Final rank Major - MBE 1918
MA 1917
Chairman Mackenzie Engineering Ltd London
Died 1959 aged 64

Captain Lachlan Mackinnon
D/B 9 September 1886 - Aberdeen
MA 1906 BL (Dist) 1908 LLB 1910
U Company 1903-14 OC August 1914
France – February - June 1915
Served in France and Flanders for three years
Final rank Lt-Colonel - DSO and Croix de
    Guerre
President Society of Advocates Aberdeen
Chairman City of Aberdeen TA Assoc 1934-37
CBE 1956 DL TD - Entry in *Who's Who*
Died 1973 aged 86

Sergeant John Douglas McLaggan
D/B 18 June 1893 - Torphins
MA 1914
U Company 1911-14
France – February - September 1915
Wounded at Hooge 25 September 1915
Commd 4th Gordons 1916
MB ChB (Dist) 1920 FRCS (Edin) 1924 FRCS 1926
Member of Staff Royal Free Hospital 1931-1958
Aural Surgeon to four generations of Royal Family
CVO 1950 KCVO 1958 Entry in *Who's Who*
Capped for Scotland at hockey
Died 1967 aged 73

Private Douglas G McLean
D/B 19 December 1893 - Boddam
Arts 1912-14
U Company 1912-14
France – February - August 1915
Wounded 19 June 1915
Commd 6th Gordons 1915 Final rank Captain
MA 1920
Parish Minister of Innellan 1928 and Earlston (Berwick) 1953
Author - *History of Fordyce Academy*
Died 1985 aged 91

Private Duncan T H McLellan
D/B 29 November 1893 - Brechin
Arts 1911-14
U Company 1912-14
France – February - September 1915
Wounded 3 June and at Hooge 25 Sept. 1915
Resumed studies MA 1916 Commd 5th Seaforth Highlanders 1917 Final rank Lieutenant
MA (Hons) 1919 Professor of Church History, Calcutta 1920. In Afridi Expedition - Indian Frontier Medal
Author - *A Short History of The Royal Scots*
Minister at Boar's Hill, Oxford
Died 1957 aged 63

Private Robert C MacLennan
D/B 29 December 1891 - Inverness
Medicine 1911-14
U Company 1911-14
France – February - September 1915
Invalided home Resumed studies
Commd RNVR August 1917
Final rank Surgeon Sub-Lieutenant
MO *HMS Discoverer* 1917-19
MB ChB 1920
General practice in St John's Chapel Co Durham
Died 1965 aged 74

Private Donald MacLeod
D/B 3 October 1888 - Lochs, Ross-shire
MA 1910
U Company 1907-11
France – February - July 1915. Invalided home
Enlisted 3rd Cameron Highlanders 1917
Commd MG Batt 1918
Final rank 2nd Lieutenant
Headmaster at Ullapool 1913
Died 1956 aged 67

Private John A MacLeod
D/B 23 December 1888 - Barvas, Lewis
MA 1910
U Company 1914
France – February - August 1915
Wounded - Discharged unfit 1916
Final rank Lance-Corporal
Teacher at Whithorn HGPS 1913 History Master Ryhope Grammar School Co Durham 1917-50
Retired to Sutherland 1950

Sergeant Victor C J MacRae
D/B 12 October 1892 - Inverness
MA (Hons) 1914
U Company 1912-14
France – February - April 1915
While trying to rescue a wounded comrade killed by a sniper 21 April 1915 aged 22

Private George McSween
D/B
Aberdeen Training Centre
U Company 1914
France – February - June 1915
Killed at Hooge 16 June 1915 aged 23

Private Roderick M MacTavish
D/B 29 April 1892 - Tain
Medicine 1911-14
U Company 1911-14
France – February - September 1915
Wounded - Discharged unfit September 1915
Re-joined RASC 1916
Final rank Sergeant-Major

Private John H S Mason
D/B 17 December 1891 - Aberdeen
MA (Hons) 1913
U Company 1914
France – February - September 1915
Editor of *Alma Mater* 1911-12
President of the University Literary Society
Engaged in literary work in London in 1914
Killed at Hooge 25 September 1915 aged 23

Private Robert H Middleton
D/B 5 December 1892 - Liverpool
Arts 1912-14
U Company 1913-14
France – February - June 1915
Killed at Hooge 1 June 1915 aged 22

Private John E Mills
D/B 18 November 1895 - Aberdeen
Science 1913-14
U Company 1914
France – February 1915 - January 1916
Commd 1916
Final rank Captain
Served in France and India

Private Frederick W Milne
D/B 1 September 1896 - Fyvie
Medicine 1913-14
U Company 1914
France – February - October 1915
Killed at Hooge 2 October 1915 aged 19

Private John Milne
D/B 24 February 1895 - Turriff
Arts 1913-14
U Company 1914
France – February 1915 - January 1918
Wounded 1916 Final rank Corporal - MM 1917
MA 1919 BSc 1921
Farming in New Zealand

Private Stewart T A Mirrlees
D/B 22 February 1892 - Lonmay
MA (Hons) 1914
U Company 1912-14
France – February 1915 - 1918
Wounded Flanders June 1915
Commd July 1918 Final rank 2nd Lieutenant
Principal Scientific Officer Air Ministry
    1920-53
Died 1970 aged 78

Private Alexander Mitchell
D/B 5 February 1890 - Aberdeen
Arts 1911-14
U Company 1914
France – February - April 1915
Killed by a sniper near Ypres 28 April 1915
    aged 25

Private George M Mitchell
D/B 6 February 1896 - Mintlaw
Arts 1913-14
U Company 1914
France – May 1915 - August 1916
Discharged 1917 Final rank Corporal
Resumed studies MB ChB 1923
General practice in Treforest, Glamorgan
Died 1953 aged 57

Private Graham Mollison
D/B 4 April 1890 - Dunnottar
Science 1911-14
U Company 1911-14
France – February - September 1915
Final rank Sergeant

Sergeant James M Morrison
D/B 10 December 1892 - Aberdeen
Medicine 1911-14
U Company 1911-14
France – February - September 1915
Resumed studies MB ChB 1917
Commd RAMC April 1917 Regular
    Commission 1918
Mesopotamian Expeditionary Force 1917-19
Major 1929 Served in India and Malaya
DADMS 3rd AA Division at onset of WW2
Retired through ill-health
Died 1967 aged 75

Private Gordon D Munro
D/B 3 April 1895 - Tarves
Medicine 1913-14
U Company 1913-14
France – February - September 1915
Declined a commission - Expert shot and
    member of the sniper section
Wounded at Hooge 25 September 1915
Died at Courtrai 2 October 1915 aged 20

Private Herbert Murray
D/B 11 December 1885 - Newhills
MA 1908 - Teacher at Robert Gordon's College
U Company 1906-8 and 1914
France – February - June 1915 and 1916-18
Wounded 16 June 1915
Commd 4th Gordons August 1915
Final rank Captain - MC 1916
Killed in France July 1918 aged 32

Private Murdo Murray
D/B 2 March 1890 - Stornoway
MA 1913
U Company 1909-14
France – February - September 1915 and 1917
Wounded three times Commd 4th Seaforth
    Highlanders December 1915
Final rank Lieutenant
HM Inspector of Schools Edinburgh, Aberdeen,
    Inverness and Ross 1928-54
Died 1964 aged 74

Private William G Murray
D/B 24 August 1894 - Turriff
Medicine 1913-14
U Company 1913-14
France – February - July 1915
Commd 1916 Final rank Lieutenant
Wounded April 1917
MB ChB 1921
General practice in Crewe 1923
Died 1961 aged 66

Private Alexander W Paterson
D/B 18 January 1894 - Forglen
Arts 1912-14
U Company 1912-14
France – February - September 1915
Transferred RE Final rank Pioneer
MA 1919 MB ChB 1923
MOH for Risca near Cardiff
Died 1950 aged 56

Private J M S Paterson
D/B
MA (Hons) Edinburgh
U Company 1913-14
France – February - April 1915
Killed near Ypres 22 April 1915

2nd Lieutenant Charles D Peterkin

D/B 14 June 1887 - Aberdeen
MA 1908 LLB 1911
U Company 1906-9 2nd Lieutenant 1909
France – February - October 1915
Wounded at Hooge 25 September 1915
Commandant of Railheads to 2nd Army in
    France 1918
Final rank Lt-Colonel - CBE 1919
OC 4th Gordons (TA) 1925-28
Partner in Peterkin and Duncan 1914-60
Entry in *Who's Who*
Died 1962 aged 74

Private James H S Peterkin

D/B 3 March 1895 - Portsoy
Arts 1913-14
France – February 1915 - August 1916
Commd 1916 Final rank Lieutenant - MC 1918
MA 1920 MB ChB 1924
General practice in Hornsea, Yorkshire
Died 1960 aged 65

Colour-Sergeant James D Pratt

D/B 13 August 1891 - Drumoak
MA (Hons) 1912 BSc (Hons) 1913
U Company 1908-14
France – February - October 1915
Wounded three times in 1915
Commd 4th Gordons March 1915
Final rank Captain - OBE (Mil) 1919
Chairman British Road Tar Assoc for 30 years
Sec/Dir Assoc of British Chemical
    Manufacturers
Controller Chemical Defence Board WW2 - CBE
Died 1978 aged 86

Private Charles Reid

D/B 9 May 1892 - Cove, Kincardineshire
MA (Hons) 1914
U Company 1912-14
France – February - September 1915
Resumed studies BSc (Spec Dist) 1916 MB ChB
    (Hons) 1917 Commd RAMC - France1917-20
    DPH (Cantab) 1921 MD (Hons) 1926
    DSc 1927 Prof. of Physiology India 1929-32
    Reader in Physiology London Univ.1936-48
    Professor of Physiology Cairo 1948-52
    WHO Prof. of Physiology Karachi 1952-57
Entry in *Who's Who*
Died 1961 aged 69

Private George Reid

D/B 3 June 1891 - Banff
Arts and Medicine 1910-14
U Company 1910-14
France – February 1915 - April 1917
Wounded in April and at Hooge 25 Sept. 1915
Commd 2nd Lieutenant 6th Gordons 1917
Killed at Arras April 1917 aged 25

Private Alexander Rule

D/B 21 September 1895 - Huntly
Arts 1913-14
U Company 1913-14
France – February - September 1915
Wounded at Hooge 25 September 1915
Commd 4th Gordons 1917
Final rank Captain MC 1918
MA 1920 BSc (For) 1921
Adviser in Forestry to UN 1951
Director Forest and Timber Bureau Canberra
    1957-60
Author *Students Under Arms* and *Forests of
    Australia*
Died 1983 aged 87

Private Francis Rumbles

D/B 17 March 1890 - Deskford, Cullen
MA 1914
U Company 1914
France – February 1915 - February 1916
Final rank Sergeant
Headmaster Breconbeds School from 1922
Died 1962 aged 72

Private George K Saunders

D/B 19 November 1894 - Shansi, China
Medicine 1913-14
U Company 1914
France – February - September 1915
Killed at Hooge 25 September 1915 aged 20

Private Robert Scarth

D/B 24 July 1894 - Firth, Orkney
Science 1912-14
U Company 1911-14
France – February 1915 - October 1916
Commd July 1919 Final rank Lieutenant
OC Orkney Home Guard 1940-45
Lord Lieutenant of Orkney OBE 1943 DL 1944 JP
Entry in *Who's Who*
Died 1966 aged 71

Lance-Corporal L C Scott

D/B
MA (Hons) Edinburgh - Divinity student
U Company 1914
France – February - March 1915
Killed by a sniper near Ypres 16 March 1915
    aged 22

Private John W Shanks

D/B 4 June 1893 - Aberdeen
Arts 1912-14
U Company 1914
France – February - September 1915
Wounded 3 June 1915
Killed at Hooge 25 September 1915 aged 22

Private William F Shearer
D/B 4 October 1895 - Banff
Medicine 1913-14
U Company 1913-14
France – February - September 1915
Discharged medically unfit - Munitions work
    1916
Resumed studies MB ChB 1922
Emigrated to South Africa

Private Alexander Silver
D/B 14 September 1894 - Kinneff, Kincardineshire
Agriculture 1912-14
U Company 1914
France – February - September 1915
Killed at Hooge 25 September 1915 aged 21

Private John W Silver
D/B 15 July 1896 - Kinneff, Kincardineshire
Arts 1913-14
U Company 1913-14
France – February 1915 - February 1916
Commd 4th Gordons January 1918
Final rank 2nd Lieutenant
Killed at Douchy 26 October 1918 aged 22

Private John M Sim
D/B 21 March 1894 - Cairnie
Arts 1913-14
U Company 1913-14
France – February - September 1915
Wounded at Hooge 25 September 1915
Commd 6th Gordons November 1915 2nd
    Lieutenant
Wounded and gassed on the Somme 1916
Joined RFC 1916 as an Observer
Killed March 1917 with RFC aged 23

Sergeant Alexander Skinner
D/B 21 July 1889 - Dingwall
Arts and Science 1909-11
U Company 1909-14
France – February - April 1915
Killed by a sniper 22 April 1915 aged 25

Lance-Corporal Alexander Slorach
D/B 15 December 1894 - Banff
Arts 1912-14
U Company 1914
France – February - December 1915
Killed near Ypres 26 December 1915 aged 21

Private James D M Smith
D/B 25 January 1895 - Mintlaw
Arts 1913-14
U Company 1913-14
France – February - September 1915
Wounded at Hooge 25 September 1915
Commd Royal Marines 1917 Final rank
    Lieutenant

MA 1920 Distinguished career in Colonial
    Service
Malayan Civil Service 1920-51 - CMG 1949
Financial Secretary Singapore Government
    1947-51
UN Technical Assistance Administration
    Nicaragua, Chile, Brazil and Venezuela
    1953-61
Entry in *Who's Who*
Died 1969 aged 74

Private Robert J Smith
D/B 11 October 1889 - Knockando
Agriculture 1910-14 UDA NDip Agr NDD 1914
U Company 1911-14
France – February - May 1915
Wounded May 1915 and sent home
Commd 6th Seaforths Aug. 1915 2nd Lieutenant
Killed on the Somme 13 November 1916
    aged 27
(Known to his friends as 'Knockando')

Private Arthur P Spark
D/B 4 June 1894 - Durris
Medicine 1911-14
U Company 1909-14
France – February - May 1915
Wounded and Commd 7th Gordons July 1915
Resumed studies MB ChB 1917 RN 1917
Final rank Surg-Lieut
Played for Scotland in war-time rugby
    international
Represented Great Britain in 1924 Paris
    Olympics
Represented British Empire in USA 1928
    (Hammer, Shot and Discus)
Lord Mayor Stoke-on-Trent 1945-50
Died 1953 aged 59

Private Lewis W Stewart
D/B 6 June 1887 - Keig
Science 1912-13
U Company 1912-14
France – February 1915-1918
Final rank Corporal

Private Robert R Stewart
D/B 13 November 1893 - Aberdeen
Arts 1910-14
U Company 1910-14
France – February - September 1915
Final rank Sergeant
Resumed studies MA (Hons) 1916
Master at Morgan Academy Dundee 1916
Mathematics teacher Robert Gordon's College
    1919-49
Died 1949 aged 56

Private Richard Surtees

D/B 1 June 1892 - Grantown-on-Spey
MA 1914
U Company 1914
France – February 1915 - December 1916
Survived the entire Somme campaign
Killed on the Somme in Dec. 1916 aged 24

Private William H Sutherland

D/B 5 March 1892 - Thurso
MA (Hons) 1914
U Company 1913-14
France – February 1915 - December 1916
Commd 2nd Lieutenant 4th Gordons Dec. 1916
MC 1917
Killed at the Canal du Nord 23 March 1918
    aged 26

Private James M Teunon

D/B 22 September 1895 - Turriff
Arts 1913-14
U Company 1915
France – September 1915
Wounded at Hooge 25 September 1915
Invalided home March 1916
Commd 2nd Lieutenant RA June 1918
Transferred RAF 1918 and gained his 'wings'
Died of appendicitis December 1918 aged 23

Sergeant James G Thomson

D/B 20 December 1893 - Fochabers
Arts 1913-14
U Company 1913-14
France – February - September 1915
Wounded at Hooge 25 September 1915
Transferred to the Royal Field Artillery
Killed on 19 October 1917 aged 23

Private Henry A Thow

D/B 24 February 1893 - Drumlithie
Arts 1913-14
U Company 1914
France – February 1915-1918
Transferred to RE Final rank RQMS
MA 1920 BSc 1921
Science Master at Dunoon Grammar School
    1924

Private Robert B Topping

D/B 28 August 1894 - Aberdeen
Science 1911-12
U Company 1910-14
France – February - June 1915
Wounded 16 June 1915
Commd Gordons October 1915
Final rank Captain
Colour-Sergeant of U Company in 1913
Resumed studies after the war but did not
    graduate

Private Daniel I Walker

D/B 11 January 1892 - New Deer
Arts and Medicine 1910-14
U Company 1910-14
France – February - May 1915
Wounded May 1915 - Spent a year in hospital
Resumed studies MA 1916 Commd OTC 1917
    MB ChB 1920 DPH 1921 Medical Officer
    of Health for Banffshire 1939 Member NE
    Scot Reg Hospital Board
Died 1951 aged 59

Private William D M Warren

D/B 26 July 1895 - Eastbourne
Science 1913-14
U Company 1914
France – February - September 1915
Commd RFA February 1918
Final rank 2nd Lieutenant

2nd Lieutenant James I Watson

D/B 27 April 1891 - Banchory-Devenick
MA 1912 - 3rd year Medicine 1914
U Company 1909-14
France – February - October 1915
Wounded at Hooge 25 September 1915
Resumed studies MB ChB 1917 Commd RAMC
General practice in Dufftown and Nairn
    1920-58
Died 1970 aged 79

Lance-Corporal James Whyte

D/B 3 May 1894 - Tarves
Arts 1912-14
U Company 1913-14
France – February - June 1915
Killed near Ypres 18 June 1915 aged 21

Private James Will

D/B 1 October 1894 - Newmill, Kincardine
Arts 1913-14
U Company 1913-14
France – February 1915 - August 1917
Killed 5 August 1917 aged 22

Private Robert Wilson

D/B 20 August 1892 - Auchnagatt
Arts 1911-14
U Company 1911-14
France – February - September 1915
POW at Hooge 25 September 1915
MA 1919 BD 1921
Assistant Minister West Parish Church Aberdeen
    Parish Minister at Udny, Perth, Eskdalemuir,
    Dumfries 1922-55 East Church, Forfar
    1955-62
Died 1967 aged 75

Private John Wood
D/B 4 March 1894 - Portknockie
Arts 1914
U Company 1914
France – February - May 1915
Commd Gordons May 1915 - Served France
    and Africa
Final rank Lieutenant
MA 1920
Entered the Ministry and held charges in Assam
    1926 Calcutta 1933-45 and Belford Church
    Edinburgh 1955
Died 1963 aged 69

BIBLIOGRAPHY

Aberdeen Daily Journal

Aberdeen University Review

Alma Mater

Banffshire Advertiser

Banffshire Herald

Bedfordshire Times and Independent

The Times

Student and Sniper-Sergeant. A Memoir of J K Forbes. (Aberdeen 1916)

With the Gordons at Ypres. Reverend A M MacLean. (Paisley 1916)

Temporary Heroes. Cecil Sommers. (London 1917)

Alma Mater Memorial Number. Vol II. (Aberdeen 1919)

History of the 51st Highland Division. F W Bewsher. (London 1921)

University of Aberdeen Roll of Service in the Great War. Mabel Allardyce. (Aberdeen 1921)

The Sixth Gordons in France and Flanders. Captain David MacKenzie. (Aberdeen 1922)

The Storm of Steel. Ernst Jünger. (London 1929)

Students Under Arms. Alexander Rule. (Aberdeen 1934)

Roll of Graduates 1901-1925. Theodore Watt. (Aberdeen 1935)

George Adam Smith. Lilian Adam Smith. (London 1943)

Tempestuous Journey. Lloyd George His Life and Times. Frank Owen. (London 1954)

The Gordon Highlanders in the First World War. Sir Cyril Falls. (Aberdeen 1958)

Roll of Graduates 1926-1955. John Mackintosh. (Aberdeen 1960)

The Donkeys. Alan Clark. (London 1961)

The First World War. A J P Taylor. (London 1963)

Fanfare for a Tin Hat. Eric Linklater. (London 1970)

Doctor Jimmy. Dr James F Fraser. (Aberdeen 1980)

Aberdeen Medico-Chirurgical Society 1789-1989. George P Milne. (Aberdeen 1989)

The Ypres Salient. Michael Scott. (Norfolk 1992)

The Letters of James Anderson. (Unpublished)

The Memoirs of Dr Walter Graham. (Unpublished)

INDEX